Stealth Juror

Trent Hammerstein

This book was inspired by and is dedicated to Julie Mehring, a courageous young woman and mother who, for well over a year, endured unjust and illegal imprisonment by a judicial tyrant in order to stand up for people's rights against arrogant, out-of-control judges who think that their mouths are the law.

If more people had her courage and strength, the system couldn't screw us all over as much as it does.

Stealth Juror

The Ultimate Defense Against Bad Laws and Government Tyranny

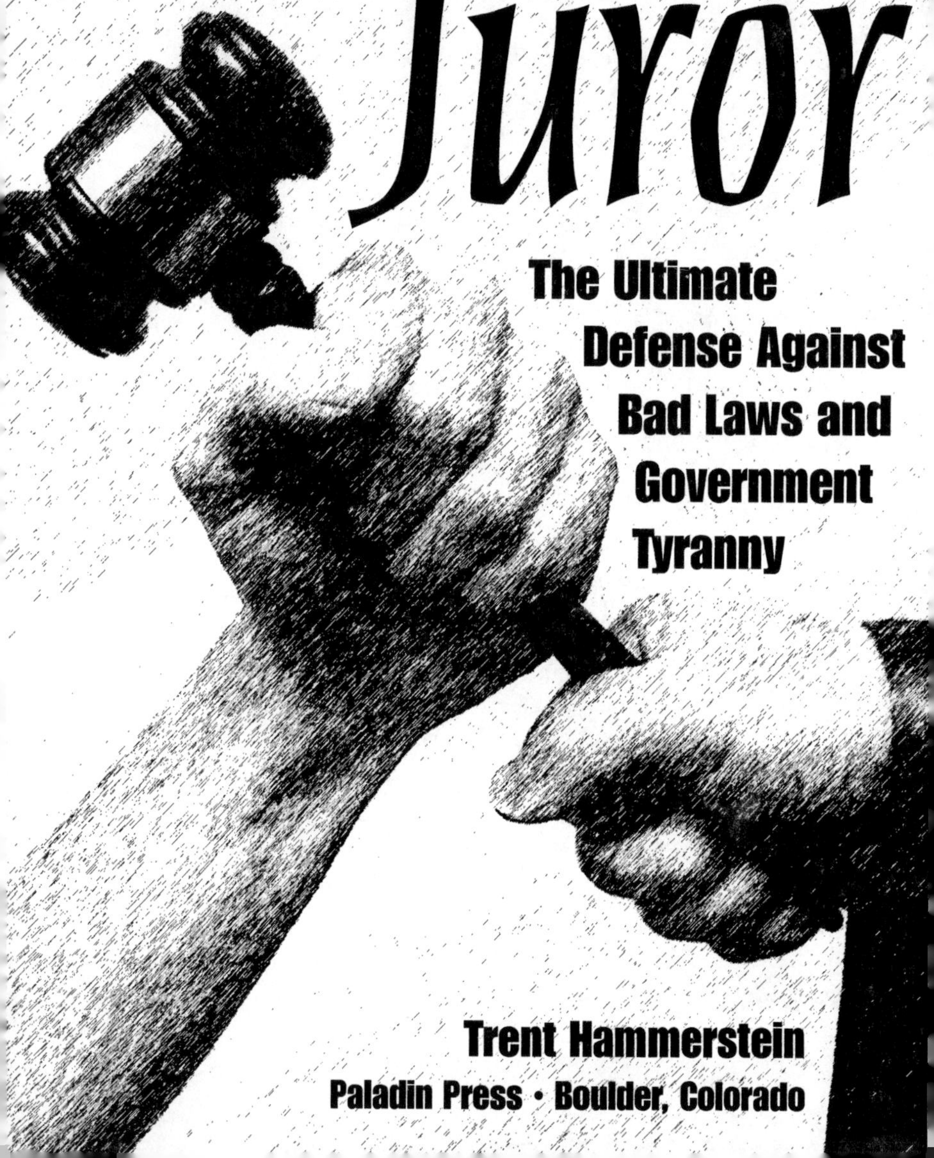

Trent Hammerstein

Paladin Press • Boulder, Colorado

Stealth Juror:
The Ultimate Defense against Bad Laws and Government Tyranny
by Trent Hammerstein

ISBN 1-58160-338-X
Printed in the United States of America

Published by Paladin Press, a division of
Paladin Enterprises, Inc.
Gunbarrel Tech Center
7077 Winchester Circle
Boulder, Colorado 80301 USA
+1.303.443.7250

Direct inquiries and/or orders to the above address.

Visit our Web site at www.paladin-press.com

TABLE OF Contents

Warning

This book should in no way be considered or construed as legal advice or instructions. It is offered *for academic study only.* The author, publisher, and distributors of this book assume no responsibility for the use or misuse of information contained herein.

Acknowledgments

There are a lot of people who deserve mention, thanks, and places of honor in this book.

First off, I give the highest recommendations and salutations to the Fully Informed Jury Association (FIJA). I had never even heard of these people until I realized a book like this was needed; then I found out they'd realized years ago that people needed to be told the same things. If you're interested in learning more about this topic, contact FIJA by calling 1-800-TEL-JURY and asking for a free infopack. You can write them at FIJA National, Box 59, Helmville, MT, 59843. If you're into the Internet thing, go to www.fija.org. ;)

Jon Ford of Paladin Press deserves a lot of credit from me. This is the second time he's listened to a crazy, half-baked idea and said "Go for it!" instead of "Get lost!" His aid, encouragement, and enthusiasm were both touching and inspiring.

Larry Chesnut taught me a lesson about doing the right thing, even when it costs you.

Harlan Ellison taught us all that it's possible to be old, rich, successful, and comfortable and still stay angry at the system instead of selling out. I hope I can stay angry despite wealth and success someday.

Thanks to the producers of HBO's series "Oz" for giving people a few things to think about.

Finally, thanks to my mother.

INTRODUCTION

The Problem with Our Laws and Courts Today

Charles Dickens began one of the best works in English literature by explaining that "Old Marley was as dead as a doornail." That fact had to be understood clearly for the tale that followed to have any meaning. Just as Dickens had to explain something at the start of A *Christmas Carol*, I have to explain a few things at the beginning of this book.

First off, I'm going to be making a lot of references to the U.S. Constitution and what the Founding Fathers of our country "intended." Now I know that may make me sound like someone who lives in a compound, has several dozen guns, and rants against the federal government. Please be assured, none of that is true. I am, I admit, not a normal member of society, but I have no allegiance to the kind of people who preach hate and plot to replace American society with something that would make

Adolph Hitler smile, whether they come from the traditionally "right" or "left" wings of the political spectrum.

When it comes to the U.S. Constitution, I'm not one of those strict constructionist types. I think the document created by Franklin, Jefferson, and their peers was a wonderful idea that had some very serious flaws, like the three-fifths decision and the fact that only white male landowners could vote. Fortunately, the Founders made their creation a true living document that could grow and change as society evolved.

So, even though I may make references to the Founders' original intent and such in reference to the Constitution, please don't think I'm advocating a return to the mentalities and attitudes of 1776. I'm not against technology or computers—as a matter of fact, I happen to love my PC. I'm not always happy with what people do with some technologies, and I'm really disappointed by the things that aren't being done that could be done to improve society, but I am definitely not a Luddite or someone who wants to go back to the "good ole days." In fact, I'm more of a left-leaning kind of person.

To further complicate things, I am also going to talk about some conspiracy theories I happen to subscribe to and believe more people ought to at least know about. This doesn't mean I see everything as a conspiracy. I don't even watch "The X-Files," and I sure as hell don't read those trashy ragazines at the checkout counter.

If you still want to lump me in with the Posse Comitatus or UFO crowds, I guess there's no point in any further effort to convince you otherwise. Anyway, I promised you people a conspiracy theory, and conspiracy theories are tried-and-true sellers, so here goes.

At the risk of sounding like some sort of bomb thrower, I must say that I do agree with the so-called "extremist fringe" in certain areas. There are some things *seriously* wrong with this country, and it's got to the point where I can't keep pretending the rot isn't there.

For more than a decade now, the United States has been on a crusade to create the world's largest prison population, and by God she has succeeded! Boy, how she's succeeded! At the time of this writing, there were more than two million people incarcerated in various forms of prison in this country. We have more people in prison than some countries have people! And there's no sign of America's prison population doing anything but continuing to grow by leaps and bounds. The worst part is, more than half the people in federal prisons are locked up on drug charges, and many of them are there for simple possession—*not* for selling drugs, *just* for possession of them.

Have you ever wondered if that's really a good thing? Does it really do you any good to have other people locked up in prison for longer and longer periods of time for things that can mostly be characterized as victimless crimes, i.e., crimes against no one but themselves?

I'm not supporting drugs. I've seen lives ruined by them up close, and it was always a miserable sight. But I've also seen lives ruined by alcohol. A good friend of my mother's recently died of liver failure brought about mostly by alcohol abuse, and hers was a long and slow death. She's no less dead than someone who overdosed on heroin, yet our society tells us that alcohol is okay while other destructive, poisonous indulgences are intolerable and anyone partaking in them needs to go to prison.

This double standard doesn't even have to involve intoxicants. I've seen lives ruined by gambling. Some people spend so much of their income on it that they have no money for food or rent, yet many states sanction casinos and lotteries while outlawing private bookie operations.

When people like me try to present such logic, we're often dismissed as "pro drug" instead of what we really are: pro truth. The system cannot really justify its stance on allowing addictive and destructive things like alcohol and tobacco to be legal while declaring marijuana a substance that merits imprisonment, even though I've personally seen marijuana help a woman survive the side effects of near-fatal breast cancer. I've never seen tobacco help anyone except the scum making money off it.

But still we see the system, operating on pure "Because I said so!" logic, imposing longer and harder prison sentences on people just for simple drug use. People who commit crimes under the influence of drugs and those who rob others for drug money belong in custody, but what about people who just smoke a marijuana cigarette once in a while to relax? Is society better off with them in prison instead of working, paying taxes, and supporting their families?

Have you ever wondered if there might be something behind America's incarceration binge besides the public's best interest? I have. I think there are some very, very dark things driving this whole "Lock 'em up!" mentality, with all its new prisons and longer sentences, that most people haven't thought about yet. Here are a few facts to back up my conspiracy theory.

If the government builds a prison in an area and moves prisoners into it from other areas (including from other states), then according to the official census, those prisoners become part of the local population. This has a tremendous impact when it comes time to dole out federal funds for things like roads and schools, which is based on census tallies.

Did you know that? Did you know that at census time, prisoners sitting in their cells are counted, just like the people who actually live in the surrounding community? From what I've seen, most people don't realize this. It was a major surprise to me when I was so informed.

So what does that mean to the people running the state? It means prisons are a great deal for them. After all, they or the federal government build a prison with taxpayer money, some of which gets skimmed off the top in bribes, graft, etc.

Then the taxpayers support the prison, which provides yet another means for your money to be funneled into someone else's pockets. Then yet more of your money is transferred to other people through federal road and school funding based partially on the number of people in prison who use neither the roads nor the schools, but the politicians still get the money anyway.

As if that wasn't enough, consider the power aspect here. Politicians gain and hold power based on how many people they claim to represent. If a prison goes into a politician's district, then he can claim the people in that prison as part of his constituency, even if they come from other states or countries (like the Cubans who have been detained for around 20 years in some federal prisons), even though they cannot vote while in prison, and even though many can't vote when they get out of prison.

Isn't that a sweet deal? The prisoners provide the politician with a power base in terms of constituency size, and he doesn't have to do a damn thing for them. He doesn't have to even bother lying to them or wasting time visiting them. He can utterly ignore them or even go out of his way to be abusive to them, and they can't vote him out or leave the district. They have no option but to continue to be his "constituency."

Deep in their hearts (assuming they have any), politicians love prisoners. They love the fact that these people bring them money and power while having no power of their own. When you consider these facts, doesn't it at least seem possible that a good number of politicians might actually want to build as large a prison population as possible and will do anything they possibly can to ensure that such a population will always be there, whether it's good for society or not?

Here's a fact that supports this theory. Official statistics from the U.S. Justice Department show that the average person going into prison for the first time is a young minority male from an economically disadvantaged home who has no high school diploma and is barely, if at all, literate. That much probably doesn't come as any great shock to you, but consider the following, and remember that this information comes from the Justice Department itself.

If that young minority male just sits in his cell for five or so years and then gets out, the odds are about 2 to 1 that he'll end up back in prison within a few years. Again, no great surprise. *But,* if that same young man successfully completes a GED (General Equivalency Diploma) program while in the joint and comes out functionally literate, the odds of him returning to prison drop to about 50/50. Furthermore, if he earns a two-year college or vocational degree while doing his time, the odds of him landing back behind bars drop to well below 25 percent.

Now we all know that government operates on statistics, probabilities, forecasts, and so forth. So what has it done in light of these statistics, data it itself has gathered and collated?

It's slashed and burned funding for prison education programs while pumping billions of dollars into building and operating more prisons. Does that tell you something about what the government really wants?

Some news reports claim that the "lock 'em up" mentality is working because we have seen a recent drop in crime rates, but the media doesn't tell you that this statistic corresponds to a general drop in the percentage of the overall population who are aged 16 to 35—the "prime crime" years of a person's life—and that the statistical age blip is probably as much responsible for the drop in crime as the "tough on crime" movement. But then, the media doesn't tell you a lot of things, does it?

As a final fact to consider, look at a recent episode that took place in California. Some people in the Golden State got tired of seeing their family members rotting in prison for nonviolent drug possession and other victimless crimes, so they opened up a chapter of a group called FAMM, or Families Against Mandatory Minimums (www.famm.org). This group believes that things like mandatory minimum sentences and "three strike" laws are putting too many people in prison for too long, and they want the results of these laws investigated. The California chapter of FAMM went through all the bureaucratic red tape necessary to launch a state investigation into these laws and whether or not they were too extreme.

The outcome? There was none. Governor Gray Davis used his position and power to block the investigation, essentially forbidding any official questioning of these policies.

Now when a government official refuses to even allow a policy or a law to be examined or questioned, there are two possibilities. One, he is so arrogant that he simply believes his views are absolutely correct so there's no point in even wasting time defending them. Or two, he knows his beliefs can't stand up to impartial review and wants to protect them from it. (Given the fact that Davis is a high-ranking politician, I'd say it could be a case of "all of the above.")

Besides the government, it's possible that the *real* powers in this country—namely, the corporations—also want to create and maintain a large prison population. What motives would corporations have for such a thing? The same as politicians: money and power.

Consider the facts. There's a big movement in the United States to privatize prisons, i.e., to turn them over to private companies and let the state pay them for operating the facilities. Under this system, we have returned to the days of slavery, when keeping people in bondage (not the fun kind, either) was a for-profit industry.

So some companies are now making money keeping people in prison. When these prisoners finally do their time and get out, do you think those companies want them to stay out, or do they want them back ASAP? Given that some corporations in this country often release dangerous products that they know will cause harm to people (like exploding gas tanks and defective tires) because it's cheaper to rig lawsuits than fix the problem, I'd say the answer is clear: corporations often value profits over lives and will do anything, including having people rot in prison, to swell their bank accounts.

If private industry wants a piece of the prison action, I have a thought on the subject: let the state and federal governments continue to run the prisons, but put companies in charge of *rehabilitation*. Let them get paid to rehab prisoners and get them on the right track so they don't end up back in the joint. Don't pay for the actual rehab; instead, keep track of the prisoners who went through their program and pay the company an annual bonus of several thousand dollars for every year these people stay out of prison. Under this plan, the companies have a real motivation to run things in a way that helps people stay out of prison as opposed to the current set-up, where they have every motive to ensure that prisoners are unprepared to make it on the outside and end up back inside. For the taxpayers it would be a lot cheaper than keeping people in prison, and if ex-cons are out working, paying taxes, and staying out of trouble, it's a real bargain!

So there you have my conspiracy theory. Government and big business may be working together to deliberately create and maintain as large a prison population as possible for their own reasons, and they are using the media (which big business controls) to convince the public that a skyrocketing prison population is a good thing instead of a massive human tragedy and a terrible failure of American society.

Even if you don't believe there may be a high-level conspiracy to create a large prison population, you still might want to ask yourself if the U.S. government should have such dominating control over citizens who have fun afoul of some rule or regulation yet have harmed no one physically or financially in the process. Don't leap to the conclusion that I'm an anarchist who opposes any sort of imprisonment. I'm not. The point is, imprisoning someone is the ultimate use of government power over the individual (excepting the relatively rarely used death penalty), and in America the government is supposed to have limited, not unlimited, power over the individual.

At its worst, imprisonment is a weapon, like a club used to batter the citizenry into submission, as it's used in countries like China. At its best, imprisonment is a tool, like a hammer, that can be used for the benefit of the majority. But even if you look upon imprisonment in its most favorable light, it's still a hammer, i.e., an instrument of force.

Now a hammer is a useful tool, I admit. There are a lot of things you need it for. It would be damn hard to build a house without one, for example. But a hammer is not a magic lamp; it can't do everything. It can drive nails, but you can't change a light bulb with one. You can't tighten a water pipe with a hammer, and you'd better not even think of changing a fuse with one. Yes, you need a hammer for a lot of things, but you can't keep everything fixed and running with just a hammer. Yet it seems to me that for a long time now, American society has acted as if the *only* solution to *every* social problem is to whip out the hammer, i.e., more and longer imprisonment.

I just can't agree with that reasoning. Sure, there are a lot of people who should be in prison. I know a few. There are also a lot of people who belong in prison who will never see the inside of one, like big businessmen who release defective products knowing that deaths will result, because ignoring the dangerous problem will add more to the bottom line than fixing it in the first place.

But there are a lot of people who *don't* belong in prison, yet they would be put there if the system had its way. Earlier I mentioned a woman who went through breast cancer and the ravages of mastectomy, radiation, and chemotherapy. I saw this woman so deathly sick from the side effects of these medical treatments that she could barely get out of bed. She suffered from such nausea and diarrhea that she couldn't keep anything inside her, and this was at a time when she needed good nutrition to survive.

The only "medicine" that helped her through this ordeal was marijuana, and I'll be damned in writing if it didn't. Does this woman, a working mother with two children, belong in prison (which would have killed her beyond a doubt), while people who put out cars with deadly flaws go free? Did she harm anyone else by smoking marijuana to ease her pain? If she was already fighting as deadly a disease as cancer, did she even harm herself? Of course not. Yet the state's slavish adherence to its cruel drug laws would have seen her locked away in a prison cell. Given her condition, it would have been a death sentence. (For a look at what can happen to people who are caught committing victimless crimes, read a book called *Ain't Nobody's Business If You Do: The Absurdity of Consensual Crimes in a Free Country* by Peter McWilliams. It's a real eye-opener on the subject.)

I don't think everyone in prison is a victim of a conspiracy, but I do think America is putting too many people in prison for way too long. Right now, laws are being enforced that put people away for 25 to life for petty offenses that used to barely rate 3 to 5 years.

Maybe you think everything I've just said is BS. Maybe you agree with the "lock 'em up!" mentality. If so, then you might as well put this book down now and give someone else a chance to read it, because there's nothing in it for you. But if you agree with any of this introduction or are at least wondering if some of it might be worthy of consideration, please read on.

CHAPTER 1

What Exactly is a Stealth Juror?

I can't claim to know exactly who coined the term "stealth juror." The first time I ever heard it was on the cable channel "Court TV" (CTV). It seemed that whenever a jury reached a verdict that the presiding judge didn't approve of, the talking faces on CTV would shake their heads, snap their fingers, and say "Oooooh, there must have been a stealth juror on that jury!"

Now, the talking heads on CTV—many of whom were lawyers of one type or another—used the term stealth juror in a derogatory fashion. It implied that the person must have lied during the preliminary proceedings to get on the jury, or he or she decided not to obey the judge's instructions, which, if they had been obeyed, would have made the jury redundant because only one verdict would have been possible—the verdict the judge wanted. (By the way, such instructions violate the whole basis for the jury process, making them invalid in the first place. More on this later, I assure you. Much more.)

The image of a stealth juror that the lackeys on CTV want to create is that of a thick-headed peasant who's too ignorant and proud to let his betters (i.e., the more knowledgeable and qualified judge) tell him how to vote and obdurately insists on voting for a verdict he feels is right regardless of what the judge wants. Well, folks, that's what a jury is *supposed* to do, which is the whole point of this book!

All too often, the so-called stealth juror is closer to what a great organization known as the Fully Informed Jury Association (or FIJA) calls a "fully informed juror"—in other words, a juror who is fully informed as to the true power and rights of a jury and the limits of a judge's authority to influence a jury's decisions with "instructions" that virtually ensure one verdict over another.

So if the term stealth juror is meant to be derogatory, why do I use it instead of fully informed juror? That's a fair question with several answers.

In the first place, I feel that a true stealth juror is just a bit different than a fully informed juror. You see, the people running the U.S. court system have set up an entire radar net to detect fully informed jurors and block them from getting on any meaningful jury. If you are a fully informed juror and let them know it, you will most likely be booted out early in the selection process.

A true stealth juror knows this, and he deliberately conceals his knowledge through whatever means necessary. He answers questions as literally as possible, he does not volunteer any information not directly requested of him, and he might even tell a few little white lies to a system that lies to ordinary citizens on a daily basis as a matter of course.

Another reason I prefer the term stealth juror over informed juror is because I feel using it to describe people who do what's right and just instead of what's "legal" and often unjust is a way of mocking those who use the term in a derogatory fashion. If you remember your American history, you might recall that the song "Yankee Doodle" was actually written in 1750 by a British Army surgeon as a mockery of the unprofessional Colonial troops. The term "doodle" was, at the time, synonymous with "simpleton." A "dandy" was basically a fop, or a man who was obsessed with making himself look higher class than he was.

So the Brits would sing that little song of theirs to imply the Colonials were stupid, ignorant fools. But the Colonials quickly adopted it for their own, even playing it during the surrender at Saratoga just to remind the British that their mighty, all-powerful army had just had its ass kicked by a bunch of doodles and dandies. The song became a mark of pride to the victorious Colonials and a part of American history.

So it is with the term stealth juror. Judges, lawyers, and similar creatures may look upon it as the mark of a liar, criminal, anarchist, or whatever, but I see it as something to be proud of. As out of control, corrupt, and incompetent as the American legal system (it sure isn't a justice system) has become, there is no shame in going in "under stealth" to try to insert a little old-fashioned, common-sense justice into it whenever and however you can.

There's a final reason I prefer the term stealth juror—I like the imagery. Here we have the American legal system, rotten and stinking of corruption and incompetence, a mindless, soulless beast that's almost as big a danger to the public as the criminals it's supposed to protect everyone from. It surrounds itself with layers of defenses to detect and weed out any juror who might rock the boat or be anything more than a mindless rubber stamp for a judge's verdict.

Then, along comes Our Hero, the stealth juror. He's the *only* part of the system that cares more about what's right, what's fair, and what's just than what is "legal" or "proper." Using knowledge I hope he or she gleans from this book and other sources like FIJA, the stealth juror carefully slides through the system's defenses and reaches the jury box. Then he or she delivers a shot of real justice into a system that openly admits justice is irrelevant to its proceedings.

Yes, any honest lawyer or judge will tell you that legality is more important than justice, and that justice is an abstract concept with no place in an American court. That is the legal system's *exact* attitude. In fact, the "top cop" himself, former FBI dictator J. Edgar Hoover, once said, "Justice is incidental to the pursuit of law and order." In other words, keeping the peons in their place is more important than achieving justice.

A stealth juror is a person who believes that justice is what a courtroom trial is supposed to be about rather than what it has become—a rigged game where money, style, acting ability, obfuscation, and wordplay matter more than truth. A stealth juror is someone who is willing to serve his time as a juror instead of weaseling out of it, who isn't afraid of being considered stupid for not finding a way to get out of jury duty. A stealth juror is someone who'd rather go and do his part to make the system work instead of just staying home and complaining about it.

A stealth juror is all those things and more. Above all, a stealth juror is someone who knows, when all is said and all is done, that he or she tried to do the right thing. Being a stealth juror is something to be very proud of.

CHAPTER 2

Why We Need Them

Now that we've established what a stealth juror is, the next question is do we need them? By now the answer to that should be painfully obvious, so let's just skip to why it is so.

We need stealth jurors for a simple reason: the current legal system is seriously defective, corrupt, incompetent and out of any sort of control. There are a multitude of reasons for this, and to clearly see how badly off course the legal system in America has become, we need to look back at how it was originally intended to be.

The court system, as created by the Founding Fathers, was basically a microcosm of their vision for America itself. As with the executive, legislative, and judicial branches of government, power in the courtroom was intentionally divided among several interests—namely the prosecutor, the defender, and the judge—

while the ultimate power was meant to be in the hands of the people, as represented by the jury. It was hoped that by giving power to several factions within the courtroom, no faction would be able to overcome the people's will and impose its own. Thus, in the court and in the country as a whole, the people were to have the final power, with appointed duties being carried out by officials with limits on their power. This was known as the doctrine of "checks and balances."

Under such a system, the prosecutor and the defender were supposedly on equal footing, with the judge serving as an impartial administrator whose main function was to advise and serve the jury. In the early days, a judge had limited powers. He was simply supposed to be an expert on the law, preventing either side from blatantly misrepresenting or lying about what the law stated because the Founders did not expect the common man to be an expert on the written law. He was never meant to keep things from the jury, as it was rightly thought that they would have the horse sense to see the facts and truth for themselves.

In a real sense, the judge was almost meant to be a referee at a boxing match. The opposing lawyers would more or less battle it out, with the judge serving to make sure things didn't get out of hand. The jury was basically like the panel of ringside judges who watched the procedures that the judge (as referee) kept in check, then evaluated and decided which side had made the better case.

As even the most cursory examination reveals, today's court system doesn't even bear a vague resemblance to the Founders' intention. The judge has ceased to be the jury's advisor and has essentially become its master. He determines what the jury hears and, therefore, pretty much what the jury decides. This has made the judge the main force in the courtroom, with jurors often relegated to the role of rubber stamping whatever verdict he or she wants. This puts tremendous power in the hands of one person, and—as the Founders were hoping to prevent when they diluted power among three branches of government—power corrupts.

Imagine, if you will, a trial in which the judge openly favors sending the accused to prison, then proceeds to muzzle the defense by not allowing them to call a single witness, present any evidence, or even make opening and closing statements uninterrupted. At the end of the trial the defendant is convicted, at which point the judge not only gives him the maximum sentence but then gloats in his face.

Unfortunately, trials like that happen in America today. I watched one on "Court TV." It was the last trial of Dr. Jack Kevorkian in Michigan before being shipped off to prison in 1999. The judge in that case made it clear from the beginning that Kevorkian was going to be convicted and sent to prison and that the trial was a mere formality. She proceeded to let the prosecution do whatever it wanted and essentially kept the defense bound and gagged.

Of course, the system was going to nail Kevorkian sooner or later. After all, he had the temerity to tell people that they had the right to end their lives if they chose, and that they had the right to seek aid in such a difficult time. Imagine that—someone telling the government it didn't have absolute mastery of every aspect of the citizen's life from womb to tomb. What audacity! No wonder they went after him more vehemently than they would, say, a rapist or someone else who just preys on innocent people rather than doing something *really* awful, like telling the authorities that people should have some choice about their lives and deaths.

It sure is a shame that there wasn't a stealth juror in that jury box, but I bet the system scrutinized every prospective juror to weed out anyone with an iota of free will or even the capacity for independent thought. They might as well have put a "drones only" sign over that jury box.

As bad as it was, the Kevorkian railroading isn't the only example of judges deciding the end result of a case on their own with no regard for the jury. Remember Louise Woodward in the "au pair" murder case in 1997? In that one, a judge wanted her to go free, so he forbade the jury from finding a verdict of manslaughter hoping that, having to choose between murder or acquittal, they'd choose to acquit. When the jury decided to convict, the judge simply nullified their verdict and imposed one of manslaughter, the same charge he said the jury couldn't reach, then released her despite her being a convicted murderer of a small child. I will always view Louise Woodward as convicted murderer who was improperly let off by an arrogant idiot in a black robe.

I have personally witnessed one of the most obscene and outrageous abuses of judicial power ever to occur in an American courtroom. In the late 1990s, there was a woman in Illinois named Julie Mehring who was married to a man and had a daughter by him. The pair eventually decided to get divorced, and the husband died of natural causes shortly thereafter.

Some time later, Julie's former mother-in-law, the daughter's paternal grandmother, suddenly demanded visitation rights with the young girl. Before this she had expressed virtually no interest in the child and had been somewhat hostile to Julie, according to her. Julie refused, citing recent Supreme Court rulings that made it clear that grandparents had limited legal rights in such cases. Nonetheless, the grandmother took it to court and a fairly low-ranking Madison County judge named Barbara Crowder *ordered* Julie to allow unsupervised visitation between the grandmother and the child.

Julie informed Crowder that she would determine who her child spent time with and refused to allow the visits, believing the grandmother wanted to turn the child against her out of spite over the divorce. Crowder then threatened Julie with jail on a contempt of court charge if she didn't allow the visits.

Julie stood up to Crowder's dictatorial attitude and spent

more than 13 months in jail for refusing to allow the visits. The child stayed with the Mehring family, and Julie went well over a year without being able to make any money or have a life. According to the jailed mother, when she tried to appeal to a higher court to overturn the contempt imprisonment, Crowder filed a motion to block the process. It was only when higher courts made it clear that they would overturn Crowder that she, after taking 13 months of Julie's life, ended the standoff.

So this situation shows that even a low-level judge has awesome power over the lives of American citizens, given that this minor member of the judiciary was able to imprison an innocent woman for more than a year without trial or appeal. From my perspective of the case, Crowder behaved like nothing more than an arrogant bully who was determined to get her way and was too immature and selfish to care how much harm or suffering she caused an innocent woman who refused to bow down to her. The fact that Julie spent 13 months in jail without trial or appeal shows how little protection a person has from judicial tyranny under our current system.

At the time of this writing, Julie was planning massive lawsuits against Crowder, Madison County, and the state of Illinois. She has been told that her suits will probably be dismissed by judges before a jury even hears them because the system has effectively declared that judges are immune to responsibility when they transgress against a citizen. (And they wonder why some people don't respect the courts anymore.) I encouraged her to file a case against the state in federal court on the grounds that this concept of "sovereign immunity" for officials who abuse their power violates the citizen's right to "petition and seek redress," as guaranteed in the U.S. Constitution.

There are plenty of other cases where judges have trampled on citizens with impunity. It only proves that no matter what they may think of themselves, judges are not gods but mere mortals, just as subject to mistake, malice, and madness as any mortal creature. That's why the Founders wanted the real power in the court to remain in the hands of the jury, with the rest dispersed among three factions, in effect making the courts a miniature replica of the entire American governmental model with its executive, legislative, and judicial branches.

How did our courts get so far off track? It was, no doubt, a gradual process. Decay usually is. Perhaps it even began with the best of intentions, as the road to hell so often does. Maybe, long ago, some judges started coming to the conclusion that they, with their years of legal experience, knew better than the jury. Maybe some judges had seen juries wrongly let guilty men go, as has happened in the past, such as in the old South. Maybe some of them decided they could make things go a little better by exerting more influence on the jury to reach the "right" verdict.

No matter what the initial cause, somewhere along the line judges began taking just a little more power over courtroom proceedings. Once this began, it was a very slippery—not to mention damn steep—slope downhill. As soon as one judge took a bit of power for himself, it was inevitable that his fellows would follow suit. After all, no one wants to appear weaker than his colleagues, right?

Of course the fact that we *allow* judges to demand that they be treated in a differential way only encourages them to become arrogant and imperious. Just look at how judges are treated today versus what the Founders intended for government officials.

In America, the highest office, that of president, has no title beyond "Mr. President," unless you throw in "Commander in Chief." The holder of the office has no robe, no scepter, and no throne. There is an official seal, but it's for the president's documents, not him personally.

The Founders wanted things that way. They were attempting to separate the Colonies from a country where leaders had titles like "Lord" or "Your Majesty" or other ridiculous honorifics that set them above the peasantry. In their wisdom the Founders specifically forbade such titles. The intent was to remind elected officials that they were *not* the public's betters, as the government class in many other countries are considered to be.

Now look at how judges in America are treated today. First, they have a bombastic title in "the honorable." They can actually order people jailed if they refuse to address them in such regal terms, whether they are honorable or not. They also have their grand black robes of office, and everyone must stand at attention whenever they deign to enter or leave the courtroom. Furthermore, they are allowed to consider themselves as "the court" and not as mere citizens performing a civic role.

As was proven in the Julie Mehring case, judges also have almost unlimited power to imprison people on any, or even no, pretext. I've heard true stories of people being sentenced to 30 days in jail because they *looked* at a judge in a manner he or she didn't like. The president of the United States cannot order a fellow American citizen imprisoned without trial, but a judge sure as hell can!

There's a parallel here to a major case that's been in and out of the spotlight the last few years. The judge in the Microsoft monopoly case of the late 1990s made some sharp observations that Microsoft CEO Bill Gates (whose business practices I will *never* defend) had a "Napoleon complex" and was very arrogant due to too much success and power. Unlike a federal judge, Gates cannot have a person imprisoned for looking at him the wrong way or for refusing to address him as "the honorable." If a high-ranking federal judge believes that Bill Gates has so much power that it fills him with Napoleonic arrogance, then somebody please tell me what powerful judges are filled with?

The final straw is that judges are above responsibility. If a judge behaves in an incompetent manner that harms someone, you can't sue him or her. Even if he openly and blatantly violates your rights and exceeds his authority in a malicious manner, courts have ruled that judges basically have iron-clad immunity, which means that the people entrusted with assigning responsibility are not held responsible themselves if they abuse their power. Now if a judge really screws up and is faced with enough public sentiment against him, he may be impeached, but even so the system says he cannot be held personally liable to the citizen he wronged in any way.

Taken together, what you're really looking at is a sure-fire formula for tyranny—unlimited power and virtually royal treatment combined with a complete lack of accountability. When you look at how the Founding Fathers were careful to put strict limits on government power, can you honestly believe for a nanosecond that they intended judges to be in such a position today? I can't.

There are, I am certain, a great many good judges out there, and I apologize if I seem to be condemning them along with their corrupt peers. Nonetheless, good or bad, *all* judges in America have far too much power and far too little accountability for anyone in what is supposed to be a democratic country. There seems to be virtually nothing that judges cannot order, even in such private matters as who a mother lets her child spend time with or when and how a person decides to die, and there are no limits to the amount of duress and force they can use against those who will not bow to their dictates.

Even though the system doesn't bother to protect the citizen from judicial tyranny, there is still one thing that can, sometimes, reign in a judge who's gone too far. Not always, I admit, but sometimes one thing can put an end to a judge's abuse of power.

Do you know what it is? If you need a hint, go look at the cover of this book. I'll wait.

That's right: a juror! In cases of judicial excess, even a lone juror can still stand as a last line of defense between personal liberty and judicial tyranny.

That's why the Founders wrote the whole concept of jury trials into the very framework of the American justice system, and it is why most civilized nations that at least pay lip service to concepts like liberty and justice have had trials by jury since the signing of the Magna Carta in 1215.

In fact, have you ever wondered where exactly the concept of trial by jury originated or how old an idea it might be? Most people probably believe it hasn't been around too long, but there is a history to the concept that makes for a bit of interesting reading and helps show how integral it is to civilization. The next chapter will give you an idea of the honorable ancient roots of jury trials.

CHAPTER 3

Trail by Jury
The Will of the Gods

Have you ever wondered where the whole concept of trial by jury began? According to history and legend, trial by jury was invented by the founders of western civilization, the ancient Greeks.

Now when the term Greek is mentioned, some low types will snigger and make allusions to sheep and sodomy. Very funny. But the more educated will know that the ancient Greeks developed what we consider the bedrock of modern Western civilization—the concept of the democratic republic, a formula for government and society that has not been bested in the whole of human history. Some might say a democracy is an imperfect way to run human society, but it's at least 10 times better than any other way that's ever been tried.

In addition to democracy and republican government, the Greeks also invented the concept of the trial by jury, with two sides arguing the facts of a given case before an unbiased jury of disinterested citizens pledged to uphold justice. Being modest, the Greeks did not take credit for coming up with such a system. Rather, they gave the credit to their gods, possibly believing that the idea of a trial by jury was of such great magnitude, it had to have been of divine origin.

There is a long, complex story written by the great Greek dramatist Aeschylus that describes the origins of trial by jury. Like many ancient Greek tales, it's of considerable length and laden with tragedy, nobility, passion, and regret. It's called *The Oresteia*, and it sets up a very complicated situation that leads to the first trial by jury in human history being convened and presided over by the gods themselves.

I'm going to present you with a concise summary of *The Oresteia* to show you how the Greeks believed that a complex situation could only be dealt with fairly and justly by having the parties involved state their cases before a group of impartial citizens, who would then debate what they had been told and determine as best they could where justice lie. Remember that this is only a brief summary of the actual tale, which is of epic length. Also remember that, prior to the events leading up to the first trial by jury, justice in ancient Greece was often a matter of personal vengeance exacted by a person who believed he or his family had been wronged.

The Oresteia tells the story of the great hero Agamemnon, who, on the eve of the decisive battle in the Trojan War between Greece and Troy, prays to the gods of Greece to intercede on behalf of his army. The denizens of Mount Olympus choose to respond to Agamemnon's plea, offering to ensure not only victory for the Greek army but a triumph without loss. In return, they ask a terrible price—the life of Agamemnon's daughter, Iphigeneia.

Being a hero and patriot, Agamemnon realizes that no one life, no matter how dear to him, can be placed above the survival of Greece itself or the lives of the thousands of loyal soldiers who have placed their faith in his leadership. He sadly sacrifices his daughter to the gods, and the Greek army defeats the Trojans the following day without the loss of a single soldier.

Tragically for Agamemnon, his sorrows have only begun, for his wife, Clytemnestra, has long sought his death so that she could inherit his wealth and power. She accuses Agamemnon of murdering her daughter and claims the right to take his life in just vengeance. After some scheming and plotting, she maneuvers the crushed hero into some other actions that "justify" her killing him, despite the fact that at heart her acts are nothing but cold-blooded, premeditated murder. In fact, one of her grounds for taking Agamemnon's life was that he had been unfaithful to her while away from home on campaign, despite the fact that she was keeping a lover named Aegisthus.

So Clytemnestra slays her husband and takes his wealth and power as she had long schemed to do under the guise of a betrayed wife and grieving mother exacting just vengeance. And she and Aegisthus may have lived happily ever after were it not for the intercession of the god Apollo and her own son, Orestes.

Orestes had suffered much by this time, between the loss of his dear sister and father, and Apollo only brings him more woe by telling him the truth about his mother's actions and motivations. After explaining all to the young Orestes, Apollo tells him that his father's spirit must have justice to find peace.

Realizing that his mother is a schemer, a betrayer, an adulteress, a hypocrite, and a murderess, Orestes kills both her and her lover. As Clytemnestra dies at her son's hand, she calls upon the Furies to take vengeance on him. The Furies were female spirits who embodied the concept of vengeance, and it was said that a wronged or dying person could call upon them to take vengeance on their behalf since, at the time, justice and revenge were pretty much the same thing. As to their temperament, one could surmise that the saying, "Hell hath no fury as a woman scorned," may trace back to them.

Believing that matricide was such a heinous act that nothing could excuse it, the Furies set out after Orestes, intent on wreaking unspeakable torment on him. But once again, Apollo interceded. Being one of the greatest of the gods, he was able to keep them from harming Orestes, but the Furies were relentless and implacable. They vowed to hunt the mortal through his life and beyond, swearing to pursue his soul even after he died.

While his godly might could thwart the Furies, Apollo could not drive them away entirely, so he was faced with the choice of protecting Orestes' body and soul through all eternity, abandoning him to his fate, or finding a third option. Not willing to abandon Orestes or spend forever protecting him, Apollo decided to consult with his fellow deities, so he had the messenger god Hermes guide the mortal to the temple of their divine relative, Athena.

Athena was the goddess of, among other things, wisdom. When Orestes arrived at her temple, she summoned Apollo and the Furies therein and proposed a solution to the situation. She would gather together the 10 finest men in Athens and bring them to her temple. Then all parties involved would state their cases and let the 10 go and debate what they had heard. Then this group would bring back a decision on Orestes' fate. If he were to be found culpable of the death of his mother, then Apollo would leave him to the tender mercies of the Furies. However, if this group of impartial men determined that Orestes was in truth innocent of evildoing, then the Furies would abandon their pursuit.

Apollo readily agreed to this, as did Orestes. The Furies eventually agreed with great reluctance, but perhaps they eventually deferred to Athena's reputation for wisdom, or maybe they allowed Athena to sway them since she, like they, was feminine. Then again they could simply have been tired of their stalemate with Apollo. The motivations of gods and spirits are at best matters of conjecture.

So, according to legend, for the first time in the history of the world a group of men swore to listen to the parties involved in a case of a man accused of a crime, to debate what they had heard, and to use their reason to determine a just outcome. God, Spirit, and Man all testified after swearing to speak the truth, and the first jury listened, debated, and eventually returned the first verdict. Since Orestes had acted to avenge a murder most foul, he was found not guilty of any evildoing.

Orestes was probably pleased by this vindication, if he was still capable of any joy given the tragedies that had befallen him, but the Furies were outraged at first, and possibly fearful too. If, after all, this new concept of trial by jury replaced vengeance, what then for the Furies, who were the very spirits of vengeance?

But the story has a happy ending for them. Athena convinced the Furies that justice was better than vengeance, and after some hesitation they pledged to foreswear revenge and instead become agents of justice, acting to punish the guilty in a fair manner from then on.

And so, according to the legend, justice administered by reason began to replace justice driven by vengeance. It was only when this happened that people could truly live together in a functional, stable, civilized society. The ancient Greeks realized this, and thus they made trials a cornerstone of their republic and attributed their origins to the gods themselves.

The full story of Orestes is quite complex, as even a concise summary shows, but it is important to grasp the underlying principles and how they relate to justice. We have a case of a young man committing what is surely one of the most heinous and abhorrent acts imaginable, the willful killing of his own mother. To the spirits of vengeance, such an act is inexcusable and worthy of retribution, but vengeance is incapable of creating true justice due to the mitigating circumstances of the situation. In the end, justice is only served by the entire case being heard by an impartial panel of fine men who become familiar, through the testimony of all involved, not only with the crime itself but the facts behind it. Only reason, supported and fueled by knowledge of the entire situation, could determine justice in such a complex situation as that of Orestes.

So the tale of Orestes not only lays the groundwork for impartial and reasoned deliberation replacing retribution and revenge but also reveals that simply knowing what someone has done is insufficient to reach a just verdict. The whole story must be known to those determining the outcome of the case because only with full knowledge can justice be served.

And that, reader, is one of the greatest failings of the modern court system. All too often the jury in an American courtroom does *not* receive full knowledge of the facts it needs to reach a just verdict. Far too often they only hear the facts the judge wants them to hear, and all too often these facts support the side of the modern equivalent of the Furies: an overzealous prosecutor.

So we see that one of the major influences on Western civilization, Ancient Greece, understood that justice was an essential part of society and hence made jury trials a part of their culture and thus their value system. You could also say they believed that a fair trial by jury was, in fact, not merely a good idea but actually the will of the Gods themselves. Think about that the next time you get called to serve on a jury.

CHAPTER 4

The Risks and Rewards of Being a Stealth Juror

Before I give you the information you'll need to become a stealth juror if you ever have the opportunity and desire, there is one issue we must deal with first. Being a stealth juror can—even though it should not—entail some risks.

I try to be an ethical person whenever possible. As such, before I offer any information, my ethics compel me to make people aware of any possible risks that acting on this information might present. So before I tell how you can become a stealth juror, I have to make certain you understand the full situation, including the possible consequences, some of which can be quite serious.

The first thing you'll risk by becoming a stealth juror is your reputation. Jurors get an awful amount of abuse in this country. Stand-up comedians (many of whom only look funny) make snide jokes about having your fate decided by "12 people too stupid to get out of jury duty."

In an incredible coincidence, one of America's most popular comic strips, "Dilbert," ran a week-long series about jury duty at the exact same time I was discussing the initial outline of this book with my editor. In the series, jurors were portrayed as idiots, genetic defects, and such. One of them literally had a hole through his head; another slept, drooled, and snored through the trial. All in all, the strip reflected the popular opinion of jurors and was an insult to anyone who's ever served on a jury.

I suppose it's largely a cultural thing. In today's society, hedonism is held up as a virtue, along with selfishness, impatience, and being as abusive as possible to those who aren't "cool." In such a society, I guess it's quite natural to look upon any inconvenience as something to avoid like the plague, so naturally jury duty is treated as something to dodge and looked upon as a stigma if you can't.

There are other risks too. Jury duty often pays very, very little, even less than a minimum-wage job, and many Americans, living from paycheck to paycheck, literally cannot afford to miss a week's salary. The jury in the criminal trial against O.J. Simpson missed more than six months of work and were paid $5 a day. A person could not even eat on that meager amount today, let alone pay his mortgage with it. As if that wasn't bad enough, in some states juries are paid even less, like less than $1 a day. It may very well be that jury duty could be an utter disaster for you financially. If that's the case, no one can really blame you for ditching it if you can.

There is an even bigger risk to being a stealth juror, though. Let me tell you the story of a woman named Laura Kriho. Ms. Kriho was a citizen in Colorado who, in 1996, answered the call to appear for jury duty. The case involved a person who was facing a long prison sentence for a nonviolent drug possession charge.

Ms. Kriho's sense of justice told her that this person did not deserve to serve a long sentence for such an act, so she listened to her conscience (as a juror always should, because the jury *is* "the conscience of the community") and argued for acquittal. During deliberation, Mr. Kriho fought against the other jurors, challenged the validity of harsh drug laws, and argued that the jury had the power to ignore the judge's order not to consider anything but "the law as he presented it" (a concept called "jury nullification" . . . but more on that later). She became the only holdout for acquittal.

But this is where the story took a turn into tyranny. Some of the other jurors complained to Judge Kenneth Barnhill about Ms. Kriho's lines of argument in the jury room. He became "just more than a little bit ticked" that someone would have the audacity to ignore his instructions and think for herself, so he angrily declared a mistrial. The district attorney suspected Ms. Kriho of being a stealth juror and investigated her background (which, by the way, is an *absolute* violation of jury law and custom in America). During his illegal and improper investigation, the prosecutor found out that, many years before, Ms. Kriho had been arrested for LSD possession. She had not been convicted; she had pled guilty and was granted a deferred judgement. The charges were eventually dropped. He also discovered that Ms. Kriho belonged to a group that supported reforming America's obviously failed drug laws.

When citizens are questioned during jury selection, they are often asked about any criminal history and if they have anything in their past that might bias their judgement. Ms. Kriho did not volunteer the fact she'd been arrested long ago and truthfully stated she had no criminal record, but the DA made a "judgement call" that she should have volunteered the information about her arrest and that not doing so gave him an excuse to go after her for wrecking his case. He also claimed that Ms. Kriho should have revealed her affiliation with the drug law reform group even though she hadn't been directly asked about such affiliations. Of course if she had volunteered this information she would have been excluded from the jury. However, belonging to a group that *supported* harsh drug laws would probably not have been grounds for exclusion!

The DA brought charges against Ms. Kriho for perjury and obstruction of justice. She was eventually convicted of contempt of court for disobeying the judge's orders (which, to reiterate, no judge has the right to give) about not letting the severity of the sentence influence the verdict and for telling the other jurors about jury nullification. The felony conviction called for a $1,200 fine.

Fortunately, a good lawyer (hey, there are exceptions to every rule) stepped up and fought the good fight for her. The gist of the defense was that the whole case was a prosecutor's vendetta against a woman who'd kept him from notching up another conviction on his record. As Ms. Kriho put it, "Would they have gone after me if I'd been the only holdout for a conviction? I don't think so." Eventually her conviction was overturned when an appeals court determined the ruling would have opened the floodgates for prosecutors to go after jurors who didn't vote their way, thereby allowing the prosecution to more or less intimidate juries.

Still, Ms. Kriho went through hell for at least a year. She had a felony conviction that could have prevented her from getting a lot of jobs and denied her the right to vote or own a gun. On top of it all, after she was exonerated she did not receive any compensation from the people who had put her through the legal wringer. They had "sovereign immunity."

The Kriho case was a clear example of the court trying to intimidate jurors into toeing the judge and prosecutor's line rather than analyzing the facts and fairness of the case on their own. Even though they failed to make an example of Ms. Kriho, it's possible that the system might try to make one out of you if you decide to let your conscience, and not a judge's illegal instructions, determine your verdict and refuse to send someone to prison for a long time over a minor offense.

There's one last fact to consider in the Kriho case. It was the first time in almost 300 years of judicial history in North America—counting the entire existence of the United States and about 75 years of pre-revolution British colonial rule—that a juror was ever convicted based on his or her vote in the jury deliberation room. Not once in the entire history of American law had a juror ever been prosecuted, let alone convicted, for his or her vote on a case.

So those are the main risks of being a stealth juror. But what are the rewards?

Well, I'm sorry to say that the rewards are pretty much intangible. There's the pride of doing the right thing and knowing that, even if the world keeps on going to hell, you at least tried to do something good. You'll also receive the quiet but quite real satisfaction of telling the system to get bent. I think every real American should have just a trace of anarchist in his psychological makeup. And who knows? Maybe you will convince your fellow jurors to acquit a defendant in a case involving a nonviolent, victimless crime. You may actually set someone free rather than feeding another soul into the huge, hungry U.S. penal system.

I know the scales of risk and reward don't look very balanced when viewed from a practical, materialistic, cynical, or selfish point of view. Is it worth it to become a stealth juror? You must let your conscience be your guide, but if the answer is yes, then read on.

CHAPTER 5

What Every Stealth Juror Needs to Know

Part 1: Jury Nullification

Are you still here? Well, I guess that means you've read everything up to now and have decided to go on. Despite the risks you'll face for becoming a stealth juror—being branded a loser for doing jury duty; possibly facing arrest, persecution, and conviction; and so on—you've decided you're still interested in the concept.

Well good for you! Some people may say you're not doing the smart thing, and hell, they may be right. But you're doing something more important—you're doing the *right* thing.

Now, there are some important things you're going to need to know in order to successfully become a stealth juror. The first one to know is that there is such a thing as *jury nullification* and that it is part and parcel of the jury system. In fact, the judicial process really cannot function in any way it was intended to without jury nullification because without it, the jury really becomes nothing more than a rubber stamp for the judge's verdict, an empty piece of scenery to maintain the illusion of a fair trial.

In a nutshell, jury nullification stands for the right and the power that jurors have to judge not only the evidence in the case before them but the very law in question. If they determine that the law itself is a bad one, they have the power to "nullify" it by acquitting the defendant no matter what the evidence indicates. In this way, we the people send a message to lawmakers that we find certain laws to be unjust. And in the words of FIJA, "Lawmakers are very sensitive to such blunt, clear messages from the voters. It's unbiased information—the kind they don't get from special-interest groups, bureaucrats, and well-paid lobbyists."

The history of jury nullification is very, very long. There's been so much written and recorded about jury nullification I could go on for page after page and still only summarize it.

Well, relax. I'm not going to do that to you. I'm only going to mention some notable cases in which jury nullification was called upon in Olde England to oppose excessive governmental power or thwart attempts by government officials to grab even more power. Then I'll cite some cases in American legal history where jury nullification was used to uphold justice over so-called law and order.

The roots of jury nullification go all the way back to the signing of the Magna Carta in medieval England. For those of you with little stomach for the history of the Middle Ages, I'll just say that the Magna Carta signified the beginning of what we would consider freedom in the Western world. It was a document that an English king named John was forced to sign in 1215 that acknowledged limits on the power of the government and that citizens had certain rights and protections from excessive or abusive governmental power.

One of the ways that the Magna Carta ensured such protections was to give any accused criminal the right to a jury trial. Prior to the signing of the Magna Carta, one way that people who displeased 'is Majesty were dealt with was to accuse them of a crime, then see to it that they were convicted in a court run by and for the monarchy. Thus the offender could be sentenced to imprisonment, exile, torture, or death and the monarchy could claim it was simply upholding the law of the land.

In order to ensure that trials would no longer be a case of automatic conviction, trial, and sentence, the practice of calling a jury of the accused's peers was established. Here is a translation of Article 39 from the Magna Carta that lays the groundwork for this practice:

No freeman shall be arrested, or imprisoned, or deprived of his freehold (property), *or his liberties, or free customs, or be outlawed, or exiled, or in any manner destroyed* ("destroyed" is a reference to physical maiming, a popular punishment in medieval times), *nor will we* (the royal "we", i.e., the king) *proceed against him, nor send any one against him, by force of arms, unless according to the sentence of his peers,* (and/or) *the Common Law of England.*

So under the Magna Carta, the king could not, in theory, simply declare someone an outlaw and then declare his property forfeit to the government. Rather, the king had to accuse him of a crime, then convince a jury of his peers to convict him before punishment could be imposed.

This was an important step in replacing a tyrant's whim with justice. Prior to the Magna Carta, a king could simply declare someone in violation of the law and impose punishment on him. In fact, King John was once quoted as saying, "The law is my mouth," meaning that whatever he said was law. (A lot of judges today seem to share a similar attitude, including the one who imprisoned Julie Mehring for 13 months without trial. Makes me wonder about reincarnation.) In order to prevent, or at least resist, such tyranny in the future, the Magna Carta inserted a jury of the accused's peers into the equation. If the jury felt the law was wrong and voted against it (i.e., the king's wishes), then the accused was set free.

So here we see that as early as the thirteenth century, a jury was intended to be sort of a handbrake on the power of the state because power, left unchecked, tends to gather momentum until it is out of control. The writers of the Magna Carta *clearly* intended that a jury could and should rule against the law if they felt the law was unjust or excessive.

One of the most notable examples of jury nullification occurred in 1670 when a jury acquitted two men named William Mead and William Penn, both of whom were important members of the Quaker religious sect. Mead and Penn were arrested and accused of violating a law from 1664 that essentially made it a crime to practice any religion in England aside from that proscribed by the Anglican church. The jury decided that while the men *had* violated the law by preaching the Quaker religion, the *law* itself was wrong and refused to convict them.

This was one of the turning points in the evolution of free society, as it established the right of a minority to not be forced to conform to the preferences of the majority. And this quantum leap toward the freedom of and from religion that we Americans take for granted today was brought to you by none other than (drum roll, please) *jury nullification!* It is one of the first examples of juries being decades ahead of governments on important social and political issues. Others were to follow.

Jury nullification has a long and proud history in the United States as well as England. Long before Abraham Lincoln issued the Emancipation Proclamation on January 1, 1863, American juries were freeing slaves. In one significant case in 1765, a mulatto female slave named Jenny Slew filed a case in Massachusetts common court asking for her freedom. She felt that since she was the child of a white woman, she should be entitled to freedom. The court refused to hear the case, slavery being a loaded political issue as well as a vital part of the state economy at the time.

Ms. Slew later filed a case in civil court, suing her owner for denying her freedom. The case went before a jury and the panel, impressed by Ms. Slew's intelligence, quickly decided that she deserved freedom. They set her free and ordered her owner, a man named John Whipple, to pay her damages and court costs.

This opened a floodgate of lawsuits filed by slaves, and in most cases juries granted them their freedom. Finally, in 1783 a Massachusetts jury was brought face-to-face with the big issue: is slavery itself wrong? They were asked if the guarantees of freedom and liberty that the Massachusetts constitution granted to "all men" applied to blacks as well as whites. The jury deliberated the issue and said "yes," thus putting a stop to slavery in the state of Massachusetts 80 years before President Lincoln issued the Emancipation Proclamation.

The point is, it took the U.S. government *eight decades* to catch up to the jury's wisdom. For 80 years there were statutes on the books that were wrong yet were still considered "the law of the land." In that time, if you let a judge instruct you to come to a verdict strictly according to the law instead of your conscience, then you would have had to vote to perpetuate slavery. Fortunately, in Massachusetts at least, a jury voted according to their conscience, making them perhaps an early stealth jury in spirit if nothing else.

There is another famous incident in which the law and the judge were wrong but the jury decided correctly, or at least they would have if the damn judge had let them decide at all! In 1872 a woman named Susan B. Anthony decided that since she was born an American, was of legal age, and paid taxes, she had the right to vote despite laws forbidding women to do so based on Christian views regarding a "woman's place." She went to her local election board and stated her case, and the men decided to let her vote.

Ms. Anthony and the men who allowed her to vote were quickly brought before a judge and a jury was convened. The prosecution stated its case, the defense stated its side, then, whether you can believe this or not, the judge ruled for a summary conviction, stating that the law only allowed a guilty verdict, hence the jury had no choice but to convict, so there was no need for them to deliberate! The defense howled over this, but the judge was adamant. He even ordered the court stenographer to record the jury's vote as guilty, then refused to allow the defense to poll the jury as was its legal right. I know it seems unbelievable, but that's the official record on the trial of Susan B. Anthony. (If you find it hard to believe that a judge today could simply impose a verdict without regard to the jury's findings, review the Louise Woodward case discussed in Chapter 2.)

Now, the defense team was mad as hell, and they tracked the jurors down and informally asked them what they would have probably voted. To a man, everyone on that jury said they would have found the defendants not guilty, thus nullifying an unjust law and granting women the right to vote decades before the government finally got around to it.

So here we have two cases of juries being far ahead of the law in terms of recognizing justice and advancing freedom in America through jury nullification. With a record like that, you'd think the courts would have learned to listen to juries. Instead, over the last few decades the system has been treating jury nullification with the kind of hostility one might expect a skinhead to receive at a bar mitzvah! Most courts vehemently deny the very existence of jury nullification and forbid, under pain of fine, imprisonment, or both, defense lawyers to even mention it or its history.

Given the noble history of jury nullification, one must wonder, "Why the bad rep?" Well, part of it I'm certain is the fault of judges who want to be little gods in their courtrooms and make sure the peasants don't make any decisions that disagree with his or her divine wisdom. Another part of it comes down to the fact that the system wants to put as many people as possible in prisons, and jury nullification represents an obstacle to that goal.

But it's not fair to lay all of the blame on the bad guys here. A share of the blame for the court's hostility toward jury nullification must be laid at the feet of certain juries that completely misused and abused their power. Perhaps the worst examples of this occurred in the "old South," where a white man sometimes could not be convicted of killing a black or anyone else who didn't meet the Ku Klux Klan's standards for being considered human. There were many cases of "good ol' boys" quite literally getting away with cold-blooded murder despite the prosecutor having enough evidence to convict a nun.

It was this string of improper jury nullifications that led the federal government to violate the principle of double jeopardy and institute "civil rights trials" as a solution. I don't think that what the government did was necessarily a *good* solution, but I think it may have been the *only* solution the situation allowed.

Let's face it—some people were getting away with murder down south, and it was due to juries refusing to vote on the evidence or anything other than their hostility toward the victims. The Klan knew that "their" juries wouldn't convict them no matter what the evidence. As Byron de la Beckwith, the coward who shot civil rights activist Medgar Evers, told a prosecutor, "You ain't nevah gonna convict me o' killin' a nigga in the state o' Mississippi." He was damn near right—it took more than 30 years to put him in prison for murdering a man with tremendous courage, a courage Beckwith will never even come close to understanding.

It was, I believe, mostly due to juries like the ones that let white murderers walk that led many in the justice system to believe that juries had to be more tightly controlled in order to ensure justice. They were wrong, of course. Possibly well-intended, but still wrong. Once the government deems that the citizenry isn't competent to do the right thing and starts deciding it needs to force the ignorant peasants do what's best for them, you've just taken the first big step down the road to totalitarianism, and even a well-meaning totalitarianism is a solution that's worse than the problem.

In more recent times, jury nullification was given another black eye (one that was aired all over the world) in the murder trial of O.J. Simpson. What happened in that circus (as prosecutor Christopher Darden so aptly called it) was that the jury, perhaps due to the racial and social politics of the time, found Simpson not guilty despite overwhelming evidence to the contrary. It was not a good day for jury nullification proponents.

I can't hate the Simpson jury too much. I honestly believe those poor people were intimidated into voting the way they did by the specter of a replay of the Rodney King riots, where people in Los Angeles ran amok over what they deemed to be institutional racism in the court system. The jurors were known in their neighborhoods. If they'd voted guilty, some people would have treated them as traitors. Their lives may very well have been endangered. They were just 12 people caught up in a nightmare in which they became prisoners for months on end. Making matters worse, the media was a gigantic, mindless beast creating the biggest mess they could out of an already bad situation in order to drive up ratings. It wasn't the damn lawyers or presiding judge Lance Ito spending months away from their homes, families, and jobs; only the jury had to go through that. But their verdict of innocent still dealt a brutal blow to those who believe in jury nullification.

Given things like the abuses committed in the old South and the sickening miscarriage of justice in the Simpson circus, it's kind of understandable that some people might think that juries need to be made to vote the "right" way. But that would be a dangerous conclusion. The system in America is not intended to make the people do the right thing; it's there to serve the public trust. If the public wants the wrong thing, it should get it, then suffer the consequences (and hopefully learn from and correct the situation). That's what living in a free society is all about.

So there you have it—a concise history of jury nullification that goes back to the roots of Western civilization, nearly eight centuries to the signing of the Magna Carta itself. You've also been shown that, like most everything, jury nullification can and has been used for good and bad purposes, depending on the intent and character of the people using it. Yet even though it has been misused, that does not give government courts the right to declare it null and void any more than it gives the government the right to annul the First Amendment because groups like neo-Nazis misuse free speech.

It doesn't matter if a judge says that there is no such thing as jury nullification. He's wrong. It doesn't matter if every last judge in America claims that juries have no power to nullify bad laws. They're all wrong, every last one of them. Once upon a time, most people believed the Earth was flat and that the sun went around it. No matter how many people believe a wrong thing, it is still a wrong thing. Just because judges may have the power to (wrongly) punish someone for disagreeing with their views, it does not make those views right. It simply makes them people who are wrong and happen to occupy positions of power.

Remember these things when you're in a jury box and a judge is telling what you "must' or "cannot" do. Never forget that *you* decide the case, not him. If he thinks or acts or says otherwise, he's wrong.

I began this chapter by quoting from an ancient document that laid the groundwork for jury nullification as a defense against tyranny. It seems fitting to my sense of symmetry to cite some more recent quotes at the end of the chapter.

In 1969, in the case of *U.S. v. Moylan*, several Vietnam War protestors were convicted for acts of opposition toward a war they believed was illegal, immoral, and unjust. They appealed to the U.S. Fourth Circuit Court of Appeals, and in a unanimous ruling, Judge Simon Sobeloff wrote this:

"If the jury feels that the law under which the defendant is accused is unjust, or that exigent circumstances justified the actions of the accused, or for any reason that appeals to their logic or passion, the jury has the power to acquit, and the courts must abide by the decision."

Unfortunately, Judge Sobeloff later caved in to fears of "jury anarchy" and ruled that juries should not be informed of this power by the courts or the lawyers for the defense. So essentially the Fourth Circuit Court of Appeals, in wrapping up *U.S. v. Moylan*, ruled that juries have the right to nullify, and it is occasionally a good thing for them to do, but they must not be *encouraged* to nullify by being informed they have that power lest it lead to lawlessness! It was hoped that by not informing juries about nullification, they would only come up with it on their own in cases where the prosecution or the law was clearly and blatantly egregious and unjust.

Some might consider that a contradictory ruling, and I tend to agree. Then again, it's probably a measure of how arrogant judges have became that they feel their verdicts don't have to make sense to the public.

Still, sometimes even the Supreme Court (What a pompous title! No wonder they're arrogant!) has ruled that juries are necessary to protect the rights of the public against laws *or* judges that are excessive. In the 1968 case of *Duncan v. Louisiana*, Supreme Court Justice Byron White, writing for the majority (winning) opinion, stated:

"The guarantee of jury trial in the federal and state constitutions reflects a profound judgement about the way in which law should be enforced and justice administered. A right to a jury trial is granted to criminal defendants in order to prevent oppression by the government. Those who wrote our constitution knew from experience that it was necessary to protect against unfounded criminal

charges brought to eliminate enemies and against judges too responsive to the voice of higher authority. The framers of the constitution strove to create an independent judiciary but insisted upon further protection against arbitrary action. Providing an accused with the right to be tried by a jury of his peers gave him an inestimable safeguard against the corrupt or overzealous prosecutor and against the compliant, biased or eccentric judge. If the defendant preferred the common-sense judgement of a jury to the more tutored but perhaps less sympathetic reaction of the single judge, he was to have it. Beyond this, the jury trial provisions in the federal and state constitutions reflect a fundamental decision about the exercise of official power—a reluctance to entrust plenary powers over the life and liberty of the citizen to one judge or a group of judges. Fear of unchecked power, so typical of our state and federal governments in other respects, found expression in the insistence upon community participation in the determination of guilt or innocence. The deep commitment of the nation to the right of jury trial in serious criminal cases as a defense against arbitrary law enforcement qualifies for protection under the Due Process clause of the fourteenth amendment, and must therefore be respected by the states."

Now I remind you, Judge White was no local yokel. He was a member of the U.S. Supreme Court when he said that, and his words *clearly* support the right of a jury to overrule a judge or even the law if, *in their opinion*, the case warrants it!

So, no matter how many people may try to deny it, it's a clear fact that an American jury has the right and power to nullify the law in the interests of justice. If judges don't want juries to have that power, they cannot simply wave their magic gavels and make it disappear. The only way to eliminate jury nullification in the United States is for those who oppose it to put together a law, or possibly even an amendment to the Constitution, then get a majority of the people or legislature to vote for it. Only the public can eliminate the right to jury nullification; judges cannot do so because it is meant to be a limit, a restraint, on their power. In America, no one is supposed to be able to arbitrarily determine what the limits of his own power are to be.

Finally, there are those who feel that "the law" should be an absolute, like the law of gravity, and not be subject to review or limitation by those it is meant to control. They feel the law should be above concerns for public opinion. To them, I offer the following quote by Wendell Phillips:

"Law is nothing unless close behind it stands a warm, living public opinion."

For those who weren't moved by that, I end this chapter with this:

"In this country, we have three ways to secure our freedom. The ballot box, the jury box and, if those don't work, the cartridge box."

—Idaho Senator Steve Symms

CHAPTER 6

What Every Stealth Juror Needs to Know

Part 2: Voir Dire

"What is voir dire?" you're probably asking about now. Voir dire is pronounced "vwar deer," at least by some people. It's a French term that literally means "To speak the truth," which courts demand from citizens while ruling that they and others in power are free to lie to the public without fear of repercussion.

(By the way, you may be wondering why they use a French term, not to mention a ton of Latin phrases, in American courts. I guess it's because the people running the courts are afraid that if they spoke plain English, the common people might actually understand what's going on. At least that's my pet theory.)

Voir dire is another one of those noble, well-intended ideas that has gone horribly wrong due to intentional misuse by the courts in its rush to create the largest prison population in the known universe.

It's a process by which prospective jurors are questioned by the lawyers representing both sides and those with baggage that might render them unsuitable for jury duty in the particular case are screened out.

Voir dire really caught on in the United States after southern juries kept letting guys go for murdering blacks no matter how solid the evidence. The original intent behind its increased use was to prevent these sorts of situations.

As I said, a noble intention, but one that's since gone awry. Today, the voir dire process is used mostly to load the jury in favor of the prosecution and to weed out anyone who might be inclined to vote according to their conscience instead of the written law. When the voir dire process was created, it was meant to find out if a juror had any interest in the outcome of a case, be it personal or financial, and exclude anyone who had such personal interests. It wasn't a bad idea, as no one wants a juror on a case who, for example, owed the accused money and therefore might want to see him go to jail so he didn't have to pay it off! Likewise, as stated earlier, no one who has a deep-seated racist mentality should be involved in a case where a person of the race he's biased against is involved.

But even so, the process became corrupted by that most corrupt of all things, the average lawyer. Lawyers began demanding that the voir dire process be expanded to cover every conceivable situation, so long as it benefited their side of the case. For a while defense lawyers were able to exploit the process to get juries slanted in their favor, but thanks to the decisions of judges, over the last 20 years or so it has swung almost completely to the prosecutor's favor.

In modern voir dire procedures, the only grounds on which you supposedly can't dismiss a potential juror are race, gender, and religion. However, political affiliation is often used to dismiss those who might be biased for the defense. If, for example, you favor ending the disastrous and draconian War on Drugs and the prosecutor learns of it, out you go. But if you favor keeping the drug war going, the defense probably can't get you booted off for your "bias."

The exact voir dire process varies from state to state, sometimes from jurisdiction to jurisdiction. In most cases the whole process is utterly in the judge's hands. Thus the jury composition and probable verdict are basically a matter of the judge's prejudices and whims.

Given these circumstances, it's impossible to give you anything but the most vague information on what to expect during voir dire. In some cases you may be asked incredibly personal questions, such as your income, what you owe and to who, what your personal feelings are on almost any subject, and whether you have ever been a victim of a crime or committed a crime and not been caught. The list goes on and on, even extending to, on occasion, questions about your sex life. In some areas you can refuse to answer such intrusive questions, but you will likely be excluded from the jury if you do. In most cases, you can't refuse to answer them, no matter how invasive they are, without going to jail for "contempt" or something similar. Of course in such a situation you would not be entitled to a trial in which a jury might (God forbid!) rule that you had a right to resist such an invasion of your privacy.

Technically, lying on a voir dire form is a felony. The crime is classed as perjury, but it could also net you contempt and obstruction of justice charges.

In my opinion, in some cases you have a moral and ethical right to lie for a simple reason: the courts and the system they represent lie to you nearly every single day on damn near every single issue, and the courts have ruled that it's okay for politicians, police, prosecutors, FBI agents, and other government officials to lie to the public whenever they see fit.

So basically the courts have adopted a "do as I say, not as I do" mentality toward you, the citizen. In other words, they treat you like a child. It was for this reason that pornographer Larry Flint showed up in court wearing an American flag as a diaper. He felt that since the courts were treating the public like babies who couldn't decide for themselves what was proper and improper to read, he was going to dress like one. Despite the fact his was a clear case of First Amendment freedom of expression, Mr. Flint was sent to prison on a contempt charge without benefit of a jury trial. After all, the jury might have agreed with him.

I will not and cannot actually encourage you to lie in this case because I don't want to feel responsible if you end up in jail. I'll just say that you have a moral and ethical right to lie to people who have openly declared that they have a right to lie to you. How to proceed is up to you.

Asides from lying on the voir dire form, another way to get past the jury selection process is to act like a sheep. If you can present a dull, drone-like demeanour and even manage to act intimidated by the court's supposed "majesty," you'll have an easier time stealthing through the system's radar screens designed to keep people with conscience and courage out of the jury box.

The main point to remember is that both sides will try to stack the jury in their favor. As things stand as I write these words, the process is heavily weighted in favor of the prosecution, no matter what you've been told about the notion of "innocent until proven guilty." Also, it is imperative to remember that if you give any indication that you've even heard of jury nullification, you will be dismissed instantly.

If you have access to the Internet or even know your way around a library, look up "voir dire." You will find all sorts of information on how lawyers conduct their questioning during the process, what they are looking for in potential jurors, and all sorts of useful information. You can use it to act in such a manner and answer their questions in such a way as to maximize your chances of getting on the jury.

Given the wide variance in jury selection processes throughout the United States, it's really not possible to give you much more information on how to get through them. Then again, I probably shouldn't anyway. If you're competent enough to be a stealth juror, you should have the wits and savvy to get through the screening process yourself.

CHAPTER 7

What Every Stealth Juror Needs to Know

Part 3: Games Lawyers Play

So you've gotten through the voir dire process. You've been poked, prodded, and probed like an abductee on a UFO and have been found eligible for jury duty. Now what do you need to know when you're in the jury box and the trial is about to begin?

You need to know the kind of games lawyers like to play in the courtroom. This includes judges, who are mostly just elevated lawyers who think they've been deified.

You also need to remember a few things. First off, you, the jury, are the *only* group who is concerned with what's right, what's fair, and what's just instead of what's legal. For the most part, the judge wants to look tough on crime, so he's more likely to rule in favor of the prosecution then the defense, especially since it's no skin off his nose if he violates the defendant's rights or sends an innocent man to prison. After all, when was the last time you ever heard of a judge being attacked at election time for being too hard on crime or having too many convictions?

Most district attorneys don't care about sending innocent people to jail either, although recent Supreme Court rulings have stripped them of absolute immunity in such cases. Still, it's very unlikely that a prosecutor who sends an innocent man to prison will ever face punishment. Most prosecutors actually look upon such things as a badge of honor—it proves how tough they are. Plus, the more convictions they get, the better they look when they run for higher office.

The defending attorney is, in most cases, an overworked schnook who is simply too tired, overworked, and burned out to really care about the client and knows that no matter what he does, the guy's probably going down anyway. If we're talking about a private lawyer instead of a public defender here, he's probably a hired gun who doesn't care one way or the other whether or not his client is guilty and will cheerfully help a child molester, rapist, or murderer beat the rap to enhance his image, make a fortune, and boost future fees.

You, the juror, are the *only* one in that court without an ulterior motive. You're the *only* one who's interested in seeing the right thing happen regardless of the political or economic ramifications. You're the *only* one who doesn't have an image or future interest in the legal system to protect, so you're the only one whose only interest in the outcome is to see that justice is done.

As such, you should look at *all* other parties—the judge, the prosecutor and the defender—with at least *some* skepticism, if not actual cynicism. You should trust your own opinion and judgement over any of the other parties involved, including the judge, who is not, despite how he or she may act, divine or infallible.

So at the beginning of the trial, when you are forced to take an oath to obey the judge's instructions (which he really doesn't have the right or power to give), just nod, mouth the words you're told to, and mentally cross your fingers, because the judge will almost always make you promise to obey his instructions, even over your own conscience or feelings. If you need a refresher on why these orders are wrong, go reread Chapter 5 and pay attention this time!

These orders are usually illegal in any event because they are made under duress—that is, if you don't say "I agree" to the judge's instruction, he can have you thrown in jail for contempt. It's a principle of American law that agreements made under coercion are illegal and unenforceable. This is another case of the system setting one standard for the peons and another for itself and should be treated with the contempt and disdain all double standards deserve.

One game judges play, especially the ones looking to run up their conviction rate prior to an election or in a particularly newsworthy case, is the *subtle bias game.* I also like to call this game "pin the conviction on the defendant," because it involves blindfolding someone, in this case the jury.

All too often the judge will try to influence the jury by the way he acts toward the lawyers and witnesses. Don't be afraid to look at and listen to the judge critically. If you note that he seems to be favoring the prosecution by treating them and their witnesses one way and showing subtle hostility or derision toward the defense side, you should factor that into your deliberation. It's quite likely the judge has already made rulings about evidence that might have an effect on the trial without your knowing about it.

A prime example of this occurred in Texas where a young woman was tried for killing her husband, who had been beating and terrorizing her. The woman was covered in bruises at the time of the killing, but the judge did not allow the jury to see the photographs of these wounds, nor would he allow the defense to even mention the years of abuse the woman had been subjected to or to even present a case based on self-defense.

The judge was openly and clearly hostile toward the defense and wanted a guilty verdict, and, surprise, surprise, he got one. The woman is still on death row in Texas at the time of this writing. Members of the jury who were later contacted by investigators for the defense and told the whole story unanimously agreed that if they'd been allowed to hear the facts and see the pictures, the defendant would have walked out of court a free woman.

So don't be afraid to examine the judge's behavior. If it seems biased or hostile, you should consider that in your final verdict. After all, a person has the right to a *fair* trial, and if the judge is out for a conviction from day one, the defendant *isn't* going to get a fair trial. If you feel the judge tried to influence you toward a guilty verdict, ask yourself if maybe you're not getting the whole picture. If there seems to be issues the defense isn't mentioning that it ought to, you can bet that the judge has gagged them and isn't letting the jury see the whole case. If you feel that the missing pieces you're not getting might lead to an acquittal, you're free to assume that the judge is angling for a conviction and vote accordingly.

Prosecutors love to play games with juries and defendants too. One game they play is called *piling on*. It goes like this. A prosecutor gets someone who may have done one thing, but since one conviction isn't worth his time he "piles on" charges, essentially trying to get a person convicted of multiple crimes for one act. In my locality, a DA charged a kid with four crimes when he was caught driving drunk: driving under the influence (DUI), driving with a blood alcohol level of greater than .08, having an open container of alcohol in a car, and operating a vehicle in an unsafe manner.

A relative of mine killed himself and a friend while driving drunk. Another relative was killed by a drunk driver, and I was nearly killed when I was a kid coming home from a Christmas party with a couple friends who were drunk, so I know that DUI is serious business. But that doesn't make it right to pile on charges for what amounts to one crime. The kid in this case was driving drunk. He should have been tried and convicted for one crime: DUI. Tacking four felonies onto one act is nothing more than legalistic sleight of hand meant to give the prosecutor more convictions on his record. As a juror, don't fall for it.

Remember that prosecutors play piling on in as many cases as possible to get as many convictions as possible. If you feel one act deserves one conviction and one punishment, vote guilty on the main charge and not guilty on the others. If anyone asks, don't be afraid to point out that the prosecutor was piling on unnecessary charges and that you felt it was unfair or unjust.

There are two other situations where prosecutors pile on extra charges. One is when they want to force someone to cop a plea in order to get an easy conviction on their records without much effort. In this situation they'll often threaten a possibly innocent person with a massive array of charges along with the associated mammoth sentence in order to coerce him to plead guilty.

The other time is when they have a weak case and hope to make it look more impressive by piling on so many charges that the jury will be flimflammed into thinking that the defendant *must* have done something wrong. This tactic was used by President Bill Clinton's political enemies to some effect. A caller in to CNN once said of the charges against President Clinton: "With this much smoke there *has* to be a fire." (My italics.)

Don't you believe it. Sometimes where there's smoke, there's just someone blowing smoke for his own reasons.

Another little game prosecutors like to play is *"Yeah, right."* The rules for "Yeah, right" go like this. Sometimes the only people who can provide a defendant with an alibi are his close family and friends, but when they try to refute the charges while on the witness stand, the prosecutor replies in front of the jury, "Yeah, right. Of course you'd say that since the defendant is your husband/son/wife/best friend/drinking buddy, etc."

The objective of "Yeah, right" is to try to make the jury feel stupid if they believe the alibi witness. The jury, fearful of being thought of as stupid, often dutifully votes guilty and the prosecutor gets another notch on his briefcase.

Before you fall for "Yeah, right," ask yourself this. Isn't it likely that the people the defendant spends most of his time with are going to be his family and friends? So isn't it likely that there will be plenty of times where the only people who can testify to the defendant's whereabouts would be those close to him or her? Don't let the prosecutor sucker you into voting guilty because you're afraid of looking like a fool if you don't. Think how foolish you'd feel if the defendant turned out to be innocent years after you put him in prison!

Defense attorneys play their own version of "Yeah right" as well, often implying that the victim has a vendetta against the accused. It's natural to feel hostile toward someone who commits a crime against you, so don't let a defense attorney try to convince you that the victim's testimony is all a lie.

There's another game that both sides play called *"Let's destroy the witness!"* There are essentially no rules here. Both sides simply march into the opposing witness's lives, ransack every little niche, and look for things to make him or her look so bad you won't believe them no matter what they say.

When lawyers on either side play this little game, you need to remember that they are *not* after the truth or the facts. They just want the dirt that makes the opposing witness look bad and therefore not credible. In fact, in many cases witnesses who could have swung a case either way have refused to come forward for fear of public humiliation, loss of their jobs, or worse. The more a lawyer from either side plays "Let's destroy the witness," the more likely it is that the witness in question has said something that really hurt that lawyer's case.

There are a lot of variants on these and other games lawyers play on juries, but they all boil down to one thing: the people who make the courtroom their daily place of business will all try to snow and browbeat you, the juror, into voting the way they want instead of the way you think. Set that fact firmly in your mind as you go into their arena and you should have no problem shrugging off their attempts at manipulating you.

The only two rules all jurors should follow in court are (1) be aware, and (2) be fair. Stick to those and you'll at least be trying to do the right thing.

CHAPTER 8

The Five Situations Where Jury Nullification is Most Likely Justified

We've established what jury nullification is and that you, the juror, have the right, power, and even the obligation to use it appropriately. Now I'd like to make you aware of the three areas in the current American legal system where the laws are the most likely to be unjust and therefore most likely in need of nullification if justice is to be served.

The first and most blatant area is the so-called War on Drugs. Juries should look at all drug cases with an especially cynical, critical eye.

Current American drug statutes are nothing more than class warfare codified into law. I know that propagandists like Rush Limbaugh talk about class warfare a lot, but the only time they begin inking about it is when someone proposes levying more taxes on the rich or punishing big business for things like toxic dumping or selling unsafe products. Well, *real* class warfare in America is propagated by the drug laws. If you look at sentencing laws and things like mandatory Minimums, you will see that drugs that are primarily consumed by rich people, like white powder cocaine, get the offender far less punishment than drugs used by poor people, like crack cocaine. This blatant class warfare puts poorer people in prison for longer periods of time than wealthier drug users.

Asides from the laws themselves, the enforcement is blatantly classist in intent and practice. Not long before I began writing this book, a lot of people were raising hell over Robert Downey Jr. and how the police wouldn't leave him alone. Mr. Downey was a marginally successful actor with a few hit movies under his belt, and he was young and good looking, which granted him "star status." He had been arrested and convicted several times for drug possession. Finally, after several incidents, including probation violations, Downey was sent to jail for just over a year. After he was paroled, he went straight back to drugs.

If Mr. Downey had been a poor guy working at a burger joint, he would likely have gone to jail on his first conviction and most certainly his second. Even if he had been paroled after a year, he would have gone *straight* back to his cell if he'd been caught doing drugs right after getting out. But because Downey is a star, even if only a minor one, he gets out, he stays out on bail, he will probably not go back for awhile, and even if he does it'll only be for a short time.

Plenty of regular people are sentenced and serve years in jail for a first-time offense, but it rarely if ever happens to the rich. Look at former New York Mets baseball star Daryl Strawberry. How many time has he and other sports "heroes" been busted for drugs, only to remain free due to the class-based treatment they receive?

When you're in that jury box and that prosecutor is asking you to put a young, poor to middle-class person away for a long time on a first-time, nonviolent drug offense, ask yourself why prosecutors don't go after Hollywood or sports stars with the same fervor. Then send that prosecutor a message: just say NO to class-based laws and imprisonment.

The second area where our legal system is widely divorced from justice and common sense is self-defense. Imagine this: you're minding your own business when some jerk gets abusive with you for whatever reason. You try to ignore it but the bellicose oaf just gets louder so you tell him where to go. Suddenly, Mr. Bigmouth comes at you with his brain switched off and his fists going full blast. You knock him on his ass and then the police show up. You think it's self-defense because he attacked you, right?

Well, in a lot of jurisdictions in America you're in for a little surprise. Even though the other guy instigated the whole incident and attacked you, you are—Surprise! Surprise!—guilty of being involved in a "consensual fight" and can be fined, convicted, or worse depending on the circumstances. I don't know how the courts justify it; they just do it. It nearly happened to me once, and only the promise of a lawsuit for false arrest kept me from being arrested. I was attacked by someone who had to stop his bicycle, get off it, and come back about 30 feet to attack me while I was on foot. It was obvious to anyone that I was the person assaulted since I couldn't possibly have overtaken a man on a bike while I was on foot, yet the local police (who make the Keystone cops look like Scotland Yard) would have happily arrested me despite the obvious facts of the incident.

A lot of laws are written by people who live in polite little societies. Safe in their gated communities, they decide how people in the real world should have to live and act. To them, you can just "walk away" from a fight if someone pushes you because that's how they live in their elite picket-fenced worlds.

So sometimes the laws they write simply aren't practically applicable in the world that most of us are forced to live in. In a case involving self-defense, whether it's a fistfight in a bar or shooting four punks in a subway, if you as a juror feel that the law is in conflict with what you consider to be real-world standards, never fear to vote in favor of a self-defense verdict, even if it wasn't self-defense in the idealized, abstract world of the law.

The third area where the law often needs to be corrected is in so-called obscenity cases. There are times and places where public obscenity is clearly present and should be dealt with. I dislike it when people blare obscene rock or rap lyrics from their car or home stereos within earshot of other people's young children, yet oftentimes nothing is done even if you call the police. So it really annoys me when the cops respond when Betty Bluenose gets in a snit because the local 7-11 is selling *Playboy* in an opaque wrapper and starts agitating for the magazine to be pulled off the shelf. Likewise when some video store opens an adult section in an isolated back room and the police come calling—the same police who do nothing about obscene and offensive music being blared publicly.

As far as I'm concerned, free speech applies to rappers, skin magazines, and adult movies equally. If people don't like living in a country where others are free to do and say things they don't like, they can shut up, pack up, and get out, because a free country lets people leave if they don't like living there.

So if you are called for an obscenity case, ask yourself if the "offending material" was reasonably isolated or visibly displayed. If it was in a back room or under the counter, send a message to the busybody do-gooders out there by voting not guilty. You can consider a guilty vote if the material was being thrown in people's faces in some way, but think carefully before you do. Because once censor wannabes get a taste of success, they get awfully annoying and hard to stop.

The fourth area in which I feel the U.S. justice system is particularly out of control and needs direct citizen input in the form of jury nullification involves cases where the system itself has failed or made a mistake and doesn't want to be held accountable for it. This attitude was epitomized in a TV movie of some years ago in which the late Burgess Meredith played a judge presiding over a case where a man was accused of punishing a group of criminals himself after the cops and courts failed to do so. His defense attorney attempted to show that the system had failed to deal with the criminals, leaving people faced with the choice of handling the situation themselves or continuing to be victimized. At one point, Meredith's character roars red-faced at the lawyer, "You will not place the criminal justice system on trial here!"

That's the exact attitude a lot of judges seem to have. They do not want the system's failings to be mentioned in a case before a jury, possibly because, like many people empowered by the state, they feel that the state should be above questioning or responsibility to individual citizens.

There was an actual case in Florida quite a while back where the system failed and people were forced to choose between letting their neighborhood go to hell or taking action. It was during the height of the crack epidemic and the drug gang wars, and some crack dealers took over an empty residence and turned it into a crack house, attracting a lot of dangerous types to what was once a clean, safe community. Pipeheads were coming at all hours of the night to buy crack, and sometimes they'd stop to rob a store or a house for money or goods to exchange for the stuff. Literally hundreds of calls to the police resulted in exactly nothing significant whatsoever being done, and sometimes the people filing the complaints were threatened by gang members.

Eventually, two fathers decided they were not going to let the system's failure continue to force their families to be surrounded by drug gangs, addicts, and other violent criminals. They watched the house carefully and, when they determined no one was in it one day, they soaked it in gasoline and burned it to the ground!

Now remember, this was abandoned property. Nonetheless, the system went after them like mad pit bulls. Fortunately a jury decided that these men acted out of the need to defend their families against a clear and present danger and acquitted them despite the DA's ravings about out-of-control vigilante justice and the judge telling them they could not, under Florida law, consider self-defense as a factor because the men and their families were not in "imminent danger."

The jury, bless them all, decided that the men *were* in danger, the law *had* failed, and they *had* been compelled to act as they did to protect their families. If that danger did not constitute self-defense under the legal definition, it did so under the real-world definition, so they opted to vote in favor of the real world and to give short shrift to the legal world.

So if you're involved in a case where it looks like the system failed, you have a right to take that into consideration when deciding the fate of a person the same system wants you to convict. You can send a strong message to the system by voting not guilty.

There is one more situation where the system really needs stealth jurors to occasionally toss a monkey wrench into the works, and I want you to really pay attention here because I'm going to tell you some important facts about what is literally a matter of life and death. I am talking about death penalty cases.

First off, what I am about to say is not a matter of being for or against the death penalty. So if I seem to be coming out against the death penalty, I'm not. I'm just stating some facts and truths that, regardless of one's stand on the issue, may indicate that there are some problems with how the American justice system handles capital punishment.

In just about every state that has a death penalty, when such a sentence is sought by the prosecution, it puts a totally different spin on the case, and I don't just mean that it raises the stakes. Rather, it adds a little twist to the jury selection process called "death qualification." DQ (and I'm not infringing on Dairy Queen's trademark here) basically means that the jury *has* to be made up of people who will state that they are willing to impose a death sentence on the accused if he or she is convicted and they feel such a sentence is justified. Before being allowed to sit on a panel, all potential jurors get grilled by the prosecution in the voir dire process to make sure they are willing to sentence someone to death. The theory is that given the fact that a man's life is at stake, the DQ jury will be more cautious.

At first glance this might seem like a good idea, and maybe it was at one time. But there's a carefully hidden sting in the tail, and it's a potential killer. The problem is that DQ juries are almost always pro prosecution and indifferent, or even hostile, to the defense. The so-called "death qualified" jury—and this has been proven by quite a bit of data and study—is *far* more likely to convict than a regular jury, and the fact that the stakes are so high does not seem to deter them. An even bigger problem is that the DQ jury is more likely to convict an *innocent* person than regular juries.

You want proof? Look at how many people have been sentenced to death and spent years on death row, only to be found innocent after up to 20 or more years! In Illinois, Republican Gov. George H. Ryan, a supporter of capital punishment, declared a moratorium on executions because, in the decade prior, *more* people had been released from death row after being found wrongly convicted than had actually been executed!

The fact is that the DQ process encourages prosecutors to go for the death penalty because it gives them even greater leeway to stack the jury with biased jurors than the normal voir dire process grants them, making it even more likely they'll get a conviction . . . and more likely the jury will convict an innocent man.

So remember, if you're involved in a capital case and plan to be a stealth juror, you can expect a tougher trip than a normal stealth juror would get, but you're also playing for higher stakes. In fact, you're playing for the ultimate stakes.

To be fair and balanced, I think I should take a bit of time to tell you when it is *not* necessary to be a stealth juror. Contrary to how I may feel at times, not every judge in America is a pompous, arrogant, tyrannical megalomaniac on a power trip who wants to look tough to advance his personal agenda. Likewise, not every district attorney is a corrupt, biased, self-serving SOB who just wants as many convictions as he can get to further his career. There are, I'm sure, decent judges and prosecutors in the American court system. Lawyers are like sperm cells, after all: one in a million may be a human being.

There are times when the system—broken, corrupt, misguided, and mismanaged as it overwhelmingly is—can, despite itself, do something right without any help from an activist. So before you decide whether to become a stealth juror in a case, look it over carefully and decide if the situation calls for one.

While I may favor stealth jurors sabotaging nonviolent drug possession convictions, for example, I don't think there needs to be a stealth juror on every drug case. If a prosecutor is trying to put someone in jail for possessing and using marijuana that he didn't hurt anyone physically or financially to get, then I say throw a monkey wrench in the case. But if the same DA is trying to put some son of a bitch in jail because he smashed a retired grandmother's head to steal her Social Security check to buy the pot, then I say grease the wheels for him!

Likewise if someone wants to kill himself with heroin—that's his business. But if he tanks up on the stuff and goes out and hurts someone, either in a deliberate crime or by causing a car accident in a drug-induced stupor, then it becomes society's business and you can convict the bastard for what is a legitimate crime.

There are plenty of other cases where the system manages to administer justice, and if it seems that it might actually do so in yours, there is probably no reason to try stealthing your way on to the jury. While a crusader who's out to do what he sees as right may be a good thing when the situation calls for it, a crusader out to fix a situation that isn't broken is at best a nuisance and at worst a menace. So unless you think the case involves a real violation of justice, either don't stealth your way in or, if you have already done so and decided that the judge and prosecutor are actually playing fair, then follow their guide and do the same.

CHAPTER 9

In the Deliberation Room

You've finally made it to the deliberation room. Once that door shuts, the jury is (at least in theory) on its own, free to decide the case's outcome based on the evidence, the law, *and its common sense and conscience.*

The most important thing to do in the deliberation room is to go in with the right attitude. Don't you *dare* go in with an attitude like, "Let's get this bull@#*% over with and go home." Remember that a lot of people throughout history have fought and died for such civil rights as trial by a jury of their peers, and that such a trial is one of the things that separates a free country from a totalitarian state.

And also remember this: what you do in that jury room is going to have a *real* effect on someone's life, a *permanent* effect. A real criminal trial isn't like an episode of "The People's Court," where all that's at stake is a few thousand dollars. In a criminal trial, the future of at least one, and probably more, people are on the line.

If you convict the accused, it's obviously going to affect him and those close to him. Likewise if you acquit him, it's going to affect those who feel that he victimized them and got away with it. So either way, your decision is going to make a difference in someone's life. That's one of the biggest responsibilities any human being can ever shoulder, and it's one of the responsibilities of living in a free country. After all, if the citizens won't take the responsibility of deciding the fate of one of their own, you can bet someone else will be happy to take it . . . and the power that goes with it.

The rest of this chapter will deal with the following assumption: you believe that the accused should not be convicted for one of the reasons outlined in the previous chapter, and you are trying to keep this person from being convicted. I will not deal with how to vote guilty for someone who you think should be convicted, because if that's the case, all you usually have to do is follow the judge's dictates, making it very easy.

The first thing to do in the jury room is try to get yourself elected foreman, forewoman, foreperson, or whatever they call it. While the foreman doesn't actually have a great deal of power in the jury room and usually only gets to read the verdict and serve as a communication channel to the judge, it's still a little better to get that position if you can.

In most places, someone nominates himself to be the foreman and the rest of the jurors vote. I think in some courts the foreman is chosen by the judge or picked randomly, but whatever the case, if you can get yourself into the foreman spot, do so. Many of the other jurors may not even want to be in the room, so if you want the position, it shouldn't be too hard to get it. (But don't fret if you don't. 'Tis but a minor setback.)

Once deliberations begin, you'll probably need to start arguing for reasons not to convict. The rest of this chapter will describe some of the most likely situations you'll face and present some basic arguments you can use to overcome them. You should not quote these verbatim, of course; just use them as guidelines in forming your own lines of reasoning. I will use nonviolent drug cases as my examples simply because they are so prevalent in the courts today, but all of the themes below can be applied to cases of self-defense, overzealous government prosecutions, or whatever.

No matter what the case, one thing you must *never* do in the jury room is mention the dreaded words "jury nullification." This could get you into a lot of trouble later on, so keep that in mind. (Remember what happened to Laura Kriho in Colorado.)

The first obstacle to preventing what you see as an unjust conviction will likely be the judge's instructions. As I explained earlier, they are generally invalid and improper no matter how many judges say they aren't because the jury, not the judge, is the final arbiter of guilt or innocence.

So, let's say you're in the deliberation room and you want a verdict of not guilty, but you've got some little sheep in there who starts bleating about "the judge's instructions." What do you say to sway the others to your side? Well, you could make an argument that goes something like this:

"If we follow the judge's orders like a robot [this might get some people's backs up, but it might get their courage up too], then the only verdict possible is guilty. If that's the way the system's supposed to work, then why bother with a jury at all? Why are we here, and why have we been called here if the judge makes the decision and tells us how to vote?

"As far as I understand the American court system, the *jury* decides, but it looks to me like the judge has his own opinion and is trying to make us agree with it. I didn't spend all that time sitting in that box away from my home and job just to be a rubber stamp for someone else's decision."

This line of reason ought to sway at least one or more average American citizen to your side. If the sheep bleats something like, "But the judge said . . . ," as if it was the word of God, ask him or her, "Did you see a halo over that judge's head? Do you think he's perfect and infallible? He's just a man, and he can be wrong like any man."

If you use a line of thought like this, tailored to suit your fellow jurors as you read them, and respond intelligently to any counterarguments, you should be able to convince them that they have the power to make their own decisions regardless of the judge's dictates. Further arguments, if needed, could go something like this:

"Every day we hear about people getting out of prison, or even off of death row, after years and years of being locked up for something they didn't do. That right there proves that judges make mistakes. I'm sure a lot of those juries who put those men in prison followed their judge's orders without making up their own minds either. You want an innocent man in prison on your conscience? I sure as hell don't, and if I have to go against what the judge said to do what I think is the right thing, well that's just too bad for the judge."

If the judge came off as pompous or arrogant during the trial, try to remind people of that. A lot of people don't like haughty attitudes, especially from "authority figures." Use that to convince the others to vote their minds and not just as the judge dictates if you feel it's a viable tactic under the circumstances.

A final suggestion for getting your fellow jurors to realize that the judge's orders can be overridden could be phrased something like this:

"Look, judges have their own little agendas, just like most people. A lot of them eventually want to move on up the ladder, whether it's to a position in government or some higher court. Now, which judges get the promotions? The ones with the most convictions, right? Whoever heard of a judge running for election being attacked for being too hard on crime? Most judges want to look tough and probably don't really care if they send an innocent man to jail. After all, they can't even be sued for malpractice like a doctor can, so maybe this judge has his own agenda and he's just using us to rubberstamp his verdict so he can look 'tough on crime,' the big political buzzword these days.

"Now, I don't have any agenda here, and neither do any of you. So I say let's trust our own views and opinions more than the judge's because we *know* we don't have any secret objectives here, but we can't be so sure about him."

By now you should have a good piece of the jury on your side unless they are all completely brainwashed drones. If that's the case, all you can probably do is hang the jury by sticking with a not guilty vote, but you should be able to get at least some out of a dozen people on your side with the preceding lines of reasoning.

Assuming you've at least swayed the jury to accept the heretical concept that the judge is not God almighty, omnipotent and infallible, you'll need to move on to the next battle.

One of the oldest and, in my view, most tired and tiring tactics a lot of lawyers use is to cry "Racism!" when they have no other options or venues. Sometimes it is justified, as there are racist individuals in every large group (including the police and court systems, don't forget), but by and large it's an irritating ploy that usually insults the integrity of many good and honest people and the intelligence of the jury that's supposed to swallow it. However, for your purposes a more effective angle may be to spotlight *class* discrimination in the courts, police, or government.

The classism tactic is a useful one, as it tends to unite the jury, whereas accusations of racism tend to divide the jury along racial lines, with whites often feeling insulted or offended by the suggestion of the "vast white conspiracy" or some such thing. But since most jurors are of the poor, middle, or working classes, they are often quite receptive to a classism argument regardless of their race, religion, or gender, making it a uniting issue rather than a divisive one.

(Rich people serving on a jury? Oh puh-leeze! When was the last time you saw a company CEO, famous sports figure, or movie star on a jury? In fact, maybe you could work that in somewhere to prove the classist nature of the whole court system if you think it will score some points with your fellow jurors.)

The exact line of argument when working a classism angle varies from case to case. If, for example, we're talking about some kid busted for possession of pot who's facing an ungodly amount of time in the slam, how about bringing up something like this:

"Bill Clinton, Al Gore, and George W. Bush all admitted to using drugs when they were young. Now these politicians are calling for huge sentences for kids doing exactly what they did! Doesn't the hypocrisy here make you sick? If these politicians think that people who do stuff like this deserve to rot behind bars, let them sign themselves into prison! Until then, I'm not sending a kid up the river for doing things that presidents, Congressmen, governors, and even judges have probably also done!"

Another tact reflects the way laws are written to actively and openly discriminate in drug cases based on which kind of drugs are being used by which class. So for example, you could say:

"This kid had crack cocaine on him and they want him to do a long time for it, but if he'd had powder coke they'd be asking for less time because more rich people use white powder than crack. I'm not going to convict someone when it means he's going to do more time based solely on the fact he had a poor man's drug in his pocket rather than a rich man's drug!"

(Of course, if the guy in question had committed actual crimes under the influence of the drug or to get money for it, you can and should convict him of those charges, but even then I suggest you vote against the narcotics conviction to send a message about blatantly classist drug laws. Once again, I am not an anarchist opposed to any control of the criminal element, even though I'm sure some judges and lawyers will call me one for making these arguments.)

Most people know that the drug war is a class war, but they don't say anything about it for fear of being accused of being "pro drug." If you come out and say it in the jury room, some jurors may respect you for having the guts to speak the truth while others may condemn you. Win a few, lose a few. The point is, at least now the rest of the jury won't be so inclined to railroad some poor defendant on typical drug charges.

Consider your local situation for more arguments. Do the people from the rich end of town often walk without being charged for things that others would be arrested and tried for? Do police routinely stop people who are driving 5 mph over the speed limit in beat-up old Fords, while they let the BMWs pass on by at 20 mph over the limit? If such cases have occurred in your town, bring them up to establish classist practices, then call for a not guilty verdict to send a message that some juries won't tolerate class-based prosecutions.

It's really easy for any intelligent, informed citizen to make a convincing argument for classism because classism permeates every aspect of American life. The rich get preferential treatment in every field, from drug prosecutions for Hollywood actors like Rob Downey Jr., who was treated with kid gloves compared to what a guy working at McDonald's would have been for similar crimes, to liver transplants for rock and sports stars, who receive an organ a younger person could have gotten, then die anyway, taking someone else's chance at life into the same grave with his drug- and booze-addled carcass.

Remember, not all drug users are the stereotypical addict types. Many have jobs and families. I've known several. If that's the case, an argument for an acquittal could go like this:

"Will our community be better off with this person in prison, soaking up our tax money, or at home with her family, working and providing for her kids?"

Or this:

"We've already got two million people in prison, most for nonviolent drug offences that weren't anyone else's business in the first place. This guy caused no harm to anyone but himself. Enough is enough!"

One line that might work with parents is this:

"What if this was *your* kid who was caught with some pot? Would you want him serving years in prison for something that's really a private family matter?"

You could also appeal to the jury's sense of mercy with a line like this:

"If we send this kid to jail for years and years, he's probably never going to get his life together after he gets out. If we give him a break now, he may be scared enough to get straight and make the most of his chance. But if we send him up, he'll probably spend the rest of his life in and out of jail."

Some people will be in favor of putting anyone even suspected of a crime in prison. They may have bought into the corporate-controlled media's line that crime rates are dropping in the United States due to skyrocketing incarceration rates. Their argument may go something like, "The law's the law, and we can't defy it." Well, when the law is placed above justice, what you end up with is a police state. If people want to live in such a country, there are plenty in the world to move to. Don't help them turn America into one.

There's one last thing to remember when you are in the jury room. Sometimes a jury "hangs," meaning it cannot reach a verdict. Generally speaking, this isn't anything to feel bad about. If a jury cannot reach a decision, then it should just say so rather than reach a verdict it doesn't feel is right.

Let me put it another way. You have a pain and go to your doctor, who does the usual plethora of tests to find out what's wrong. After collecting and analyzing every last bit of data he can gather, the doctor is certain your ailment is being caused by one of two things, but he cannot, despite hours of diligent thought and study, determine which it is.

Now what should the doctor do: just pick one or the other and hope for the best? Or should he tell you the truth and recommend you see another doctor? The answer is obvious, and so it is with a jury that is unable to decide on a verdict. They should simply say so and recommend the case be viewed by another jury.

So don't think that a hung jury is a failure or something to be ashamed of. The real shame would be if you returned a verdict you didn't honestly and unanimously support. As for the argument that hung juries lead to retrials, costing the government money, well remember that the government doesn't mind spending billions of dollars to keep hundreds of thousands of people locked up for obscene amounts of time over nonviolent offenses that mostly shouldn't be crimes in the first place, so don't let financial concerns sway you. A hung jury is better than a jury that returns a verdict it's not certain of, just as a doctor who tells you he can't find out what's wrong with you is better than one who just picks a diagnosis he hopes is right.

The bottom line is, how you sway the jury is up to you. Your course of action will need to be based entirely on the situation you're in, your assessment of it and the individuals involved, and your skills at persuasion. I've given you the groundwork. The rest is up to you.

CHAPTER 10

What to Do If They Come for You

As I've stated earlier, I believe there is an ongoing, deliberate, high-level, and possibly multifaceted conspiracy in this country to create and maintain as large a prison population as possible. It is being carried out by the government and the people who control the government, namely the major corporations.

One of my main reasons for writing this book is to fight this conspiracy. It is taking the lives of hundreds of thousands of people and stripping the rights from millions more under the smokescreen of the War on Drugs and other Orwellian schemes.

If this little book actually does have a noticeable effect in the form of more and more acquittals for people charged with nonviolent, victimless crimes, I'm sure the people behind this conspiracy will react swiftly and brutally to keep their plans from being derailed. They may come after me for writing this book, and they may go after anyone who tries to practice what I've suggested.

I'll deal with it if they come for me. You should think about what to do if they come for you.

Assuming you've been picked for jury duty and have gone through the trial to the end and achieved either an acquittal or a hung jury, you may find that your troubles have only just begun. Some busybody on the jury may decide to run to the judge like a little tattletale, telling him you said mean things about him, implied he wasn't the avatar of God Almighty, and that he was even, possibly, fallible.

A lot of judges seem to think that they are above the judgement of underlings such as jury members, and this one might decide to heap a mountain of "divine retribution" on your head as a warning to the other mortals not to challenge the gods. Likewise, some mean-spirited district attorney who just had his track record blown by not getting a conviction may opt to make an example out of a stealth juror to scare the rest of the citizens in his district into rubber stamping his cases with guilty verdicts.

So sooner or later a stealth juror may find him or herself under attack, just like Laura Kriho did back in 1996. Even though Ms. Kriho eventually won her case, she was initially convicted and had to spend a great deal of time and money getting it overturned. I assure you, the state did not compensate her for her troubles. As for those who brought the charges against her, it wasn't *their* money they were spending, now was it?

If they do come after you, you must launch an effective and aggressive defense right away. And the two most important, immediate steps are to (1) say *nothing* to any police officer, prosecutor, or judge, invoking your Fifth Amendment right to remain silent if necessary, and (2) get a good lawyer pronto. You will be facing a system with virtually unlimited power and resources that is out to nail your hide to a cross as a warning to the other uppity peasants. It is in your best interests to keep your mouth shut so you do not incriminate yourself accidentally, and it is important to get as good a lawyer as you can afford to come out of the situation intact. Be wary of hiring your brother-in-law the attorney who specializes in DUIs and divorces. He most likely will be in over his head, and it is you who will pay the price for it, not him. Find someone with experience in these matters.

If you cannot afford to hire your own attorney, there are several organizations you may be able to turn to for help. Please note that these groups are high-profile defenders of justice, and as such they are inundated with requests for legal representation. Even if they wanted to, they simply do not have the time or the resources to take on every case thrust in front of them, no matter how egregious the injustice. Do not be afraid to approach them if you have a strong case, but do not be surprised if you are turned down. Always be prepared to hire an attorney on your own.

The first thing to do is contact the Fully Informed Jury Alliance at www.fija.org, explain the situation, and ask for help. These people will be happy to direct you to all the aid they can, including a detailed description of the Laura Kriho case, the transcripts from her trial, and the judge's final ruling acquitting her and condemning the practice of going after jurors who render the "wrong" verdict.

Another source of aid could be the American Civil Liberties Union, better known as the ACLU. Regardless of how you feel about them, they may very well come to the aid of a citizen who was being persecuted (no, I did not mean to say "prosecuted") for exercising his or her right to nullify in the interests of justice. The ACLU helps neo-Nazis demonstrate in Jewish neighborhoods; they will help you if you have a solid case for the right of jury power as a buffer against excessive authority.

A lesser known organization is the relatively new Institute

of Justice (www.ij.org). Founded in 1991, the IJ's Web site describes itself as "a civil liberties law firm" that "pursues cutting-edge litigation in the courts of law . . . on behalf of individuals whose most basic rights are denied by the State." They are located in Washington D.C., so they know exactly how to operate in that nest of snakes. Definitely worth a try.

If you or the person you fought to keep out of an unjust conviction are of the right race, you might get help from the NAACP or similar civil rights groups. They might view the situation as racially biased and lend their support.

The next thing to do is the hardest: *don't give in to the bastards!* They may try to get you to cop a plea to a reduced charge to avoid a more serious conviction and sentence. Tell them (through your attorney) that you didn't do anything wrong so you aren't going to "accept" any punishment whatsoever. Then fight them! If you let them batter, harass, and terrorize you into pleading guilty to *anything,* even a misdemeanor, you'll only help open a floodgate that continues to allow judges and prosecutors to intimidate and threaten juries into giving them the verdict they want on any issue.

The system will resort to all sorts of little tricks to wear you down. It will schedule a court date, make you appear, then reschedule it to another date, forcing you to miss more work. Another of their cute tricks is to dredge into your private life and leak your most intimate personal details to the news media. Nonetheless, you've got to stand up and hold the line here to avoid giving them more ammunition and encouragement to justify jury intimidation.

Now, once you've fought the bastards and refused to give an inch, there's one last thing to do: *sue the bastards!* That's right: sue them! The U.S. Supreme Court has ruled that prosecutors do not have "blanket immunity" from lawsuits based on false or malicious prosecution, so if one comes after you, go after him in turn by claiming that his case was unjustified and a malicious attempt to punish a juror who wouldn't vote his way. Make the SOB miserable, and try to get some of the groups I've listed to help you. In short, turn the prosecutor's attempt at making an example out of you into your chance to make an example out of him. It'll feel great. Trust me.

CHAPTER 11

What You Can Do to Fix the System Even if You're Never on a Jury

We have established that (1) the system is a mess, (2) it is putting too many people in jail for questionable reasons, and (3) if you get to be on a jury, you can try to do something to fight it. But what about the majority of people who never will get called to jury duty but still agree that the system needs some correction? Is there anything they can do?

Sure there is. What you need to do is turn off the TV, get off the couch, get out there, and start fighting for new laws that will put some leashes and muzzles on the system before it's too late. Never underestimate the power of a determined individual. The "three strikes" sentencing laws were born after the parents of one murdered child wouldn't let it go. And look at the whole "America's Most Wanted" television series, which works to put real criminals behind bars—that was the result of one man, the father of a murdered child, who wouldn't give up.

So if you are sick of a system that locks hundreds of thousands of people in prison who don't belong there, a system that gives itself more and more power over your life, then start fighting for your rights *now* and never give up!

There are thousands of laws that could be repealed or at least tamed, and new ones that could be enacted, that would immediately limit the power of the court system to a level consistent with a free society and give more power back to the public where it was meant to be. I have a few suggestions that might help. Review the list below and, if you agree, start getting active in your community or in groups that take the fight to a national level.

ABOLISH THE DRUG WAR

The War on Drugs has become the War on Freedom and the War on the Poor. As should be clear by now, poor people are serving long sentences for minor drug offences while rich people either get a small fine or no punishment at all. I personally cannot believe that the alternative—ending the War on Drugs and letting people do as they choose, so long as it affects no one but themselves—could be worse than what's happening now.

The people in power who directly benefit from the war will trot out their tired old horror stories about how drugs ruin lives. But now the people who are for ending the war have their own horror stories to tell, stories of people getting 20-year sentences for simple drug possession, or innocent wives and girlfriends being falsely turned in by husbands and boyfriends to get themselves reduced sentences.

The drug war is the very embodiment of the raw force of government power directed against citizens who engage in unsanctioned personal activities. It is no better than the days of Prohibition, when poor people ran the risk of getting their heads caved in by a cop's nightstick in a speakeasy while the rich sipped champagne with impunity. Yet the drug war has failed just like alcohol prohibition failed, and it will continue to fail because it is based on lies, hypocrisy, and the arrogance of those in government who think they know what's best for all and don't care what the citizens of this country think.

MAKE "THREE STRIKES" LAWS SENSIBLE, OR ELIMINATE THEM

I have respect for those people who originally championed the "three strikes" sentencing laws. At least they got up and did something instead of just letting themselves be victims, and I can understand why those laws must have looked quite appealing at first.

However, while the concept may have been somewhat sound in theory, its execution has been grossly flawed. Now people are being sentenced to 25 years to life in prison for trivial offences! There was a case where a person was given a third strike (and therefore a long prison sentence) for swiping a slice of pizza off a store counter. As I was writing this, another man was facing 25 years for taking a couple of coins off the dashboard of a car the owner had left open. The amount was less that $1, but he's still looking at a quarter of a century in prison!

At the very least, I believe the three-strikes laws have been implemented poorly. I also believe they possess a subtle flaw in their very nature that makes them questionable at best. The flaw is this: these laws make the assumption that the judge is not competent to determine a fair sentence and must, therefore, be told how to sentence someone. I have a huge problem with this for one reason: if the judge is assumed to be unable to make a proper determination as to sentencing, how can he or she be competent enough to determine first and second strike sentences as many judges often do? The three strikes laws do nothing to curtail a judge's power to determine the verdict by screening and directing the jury beforehand, excluding evidence that might lead to a "wrong" verdict, and so on, but they prevent them from assigning appropriate punishments to minor offences. So it binds a judge's hands as to punishment but gives him a free hand to determine the verdict.

Am I the only one to see that there is something wrong with this picture? If the judge is not competent to determine a sentence, then he is not competent to determine what evidence a jury should hear, and if he is competent to determine what evidence should be allowed, he is competent to determine an appropriate sentence.

Three strikes laws should be amended severely or eliminated entirely. At the most they should only apply to serious and/or violent felonies where significant harm was done to a person or property, not to petty offences with "damages" measured in pennies.

IMPOSE RESPONSIBILITY ON THE SYSTEM

A while back it came to the media's attention that a great many innocent people were being maimed, crippled, and killed by police officers engaging in reckless high-speed chases with fleeing cars. Often the chases were found to be unnecessary. The media brought this to the public's attention and the system quickly responded to the situation . . . but not in a way you might expect. In many cities and states, instead of curtailing the practice, lawmakers declared their jurisdictions immune to lawsuits brought by citizens who had been injured and the families of those who had been killed. Likewise, recent court decisions have allowed cities and states to declare themselves immune to other cases of police excess. Even if a police officer commits a crime against a citizen in some jurisdictions, the citizen cannot sue the city or state that empowered the cop because the system has simply declared itself above responsibility.

Individual judges have always had blanket immunity from lawsuits initiated by those they've wronged. In California, a judge openly and blatantly violated the rights of a pregnant woman by putting her in jail when the situation did not call for it simply to prevent her from getting an abortion. The judge openly said she imprisoned the woman because she was against abortion. The woman sued the judge for violating her rights, and the judge presiding over the case agreed that the first judge had violated the woman's rights. But then the second judge dismissed the case, saying that even when a judge violates a citizen's rights, he or she is utterly immune to any sort of responsibility.

The situation is basically the same with overzealous prosecutors. The U.S. Supreme Court recently ruled that prosecutors can be sued for egregious violations of individual rights, but they set the standards so high that DAs are still practically immune to lawsuits from those they wrongly imprison.

So we have a system where the citizen can be punished by the state through the courts, but the courts are increasingly immune to any responsibility to the citizenry when it wrongs them. Power without accountability is generally a very bad idea, and it is absolutely toxic to a free society.

The American public should demand that the system cannot declare itself immune to responsibility. When the system wrongs an individual, that individual has a right to "petition the government for a redress of grievances" (read: sue) as guaranteed by the First Amendment of the U.S. Constitution.

ESTABLISH CITIZEN OVERSIGHT PANELS TO CONTROL JUDGES

Many cities used to have "citizen oversight committees" to oversee the police department and make certain it stayed true to the motto, "To protect and to serve." In most places today, such things either no longer exist or are so politicized as to be nothing but pointless rubber stamps for the will of the local political machine.

In light of recent cases of judicial abuse of power, citizens who want protection from excessively zealous or tyrannical judges should demand the formation of a citizen's panel to oversee and, if need be, reign in judges who go too far and think themselves to be like England's King John, who proclaimed, "The law is my mouth!"

If such committees are established, a citizen who feels his rights have been violated by a judge would have the option of demanding a review by the oversight panel. If the panel determines a wrong has been done, they and *not* another judge would have the power to void a contempt citation, issue a reprimand, or take other appropriate action. As is, the only person who can judge a judge today is another judge. Anyone else hear the sound of backs being scratched?

If you need proof of the results of allowing judges to sit in judgement of their fellow consider this: according to the group Citizens for Judicial Accountability (CJA, on the Web at www.judicialaccountability.org), some 97 percent of charges brought against lawyers and 99 percent of charges brought against judges by citizens who feel they were wronged in some way were dismissed by another judge. When these summary dismissals are appealed, 65 percent are denied without comment by—you guessed it!—another judge.

Allowing judges to practice self-oversight is like letting the weasels guard the henhouse. Given the tremendous power they have taken upon themselves, judges should be held accountable to the citizenry, not their peers.

DRASTICALLY REDUCE THE POWER OF JUDGES

Judges have too much power in the courtroom, plain and simple. If a judge wants a particular verdict, he simply muzzles one side of the case and, barring a stealth juror in the deliberation room, gets the verdict he wants. (Ask Jack Kevorkian about that.) If a jury comes back with a verdict the judge doesn't like, at least half the time he can simply wipe his ass on it and flush it, then impose his own verdict over the jury's. (Ask the parents of the child killed by convicted, then released, murderer Louise Woodward about that.)

In civil cases the jury is virtually meaningless, as the judge can treat any verdict they hand down like a lump of Silly Putty, molding or discarding it at his whim. We so often hear of huge awards being given by juries to the victims of unsafe products or practices, but we so rarely hear about it when (not if) those awards are drastically reduced or eliminated altogether by judges. Likewise, judges have even overturned laws established by the voting public. In such cases they have become lawmakers without regard to the public will.

For all of these reasons and more, the immense amount of power currently wielded by American judges should be drastically curtailed. Their ability to alter a jury verdict should be severely cut and subject to review. A judge should *never* be allowed to completely abrogate a verdict, as the jury, not the judge, is meant to be the final word of authority. It is the jury who represents the public, and under the United States Constitution, it is the public who has the final power in the courtroom.

I believe that making judges liable for misconduct and establishing citizens oversight panels would accomplish most of the necessary limiting of judicial power. But then again, you can't have too much control over judges, given some of their recent excesses. If some judges don't want to continue their jobs bereft of their (up to now) nearly limitless power and limitless irresponsibility, they can seek other employment.

STRICTLY LIMIT THE VOIR DIRE PROCESS

The voir dire process has gone from a well-intended idea to a complete disaster for the jury system. Giving both sides the ability to weed out jurors has led to juries comprised mostly of mindless lumps of malleable mush that are incapable of grasping, let along adequately exercising, the power and responsibility of a jury in the American court system.

In England (a country I seldom defend, mind you), there is virtually no voir dire process whatsoever. Both sides have to make do with the first dozen people who come into the jury box, barring blatant cases of obvious bias.

In the United States, the voir dire process should be reduced to three simple questions: (1) Are you mentally and physically capable of being a juror? (2) Do you have any personal involvement that makes you incapable of being an unbiased juror in this case? (3) Are you willing to accept the power and responsibility of being a juror?

Now the third question, the one about responsibility, would be used to prosecute any juror who turns out to have lied about question number 2. If it's later discovered that a juror has a personal stake or interest in a case, then he or she should be liable for prosecution.

I also believe jury duty, like military service, should be voluntary. If you think we wouldn't get enough volunteers, read on.

GIVE JURIES BETTER TREATMENT

Juries today are treated like dung. They can be sequestered (i.e., imprisoned) on a judge's whim, as the O.J. Simpson panel was imprisoned for more than six months. Jurors are rarely paid anything above a pittance, and many can't afford to miss all of the time at their jobs that is required to serve on a jury.

Jurors should be paid a minimum of $50 per day or an amount equal to their net income loss, whichever is greater. That alone would make jury duty possible for many workaday types who need their income to get by. Also, the practice of imprisoning juries should be strictly limited and should only be possible with the jury's permission. The judge should not be able to impose such a situation on them without convincing them it is necessary or in their best interests.

Finally, jurors should be allowed to write out questions and submit them to the judge to be asked of any witness they choose. The judge should be required to ask the questions impartially. This would drastically empower juries and disempower the judge's and lawyers' ability to solely direct the proceedings.

OUTLAW PLEA BARGAINS

Plea bargains serve no useful purpose in the American justice system and in fact are mostly counterproductive to justice. All too often, a plea bargain is a devil's deal struck between a guilty man and an overworked prosecutor. The guilty man benefits by getting a sentence far lower than he deserved, and the DA gets an easy win for his record that boosts his ratings. Who loses in the deal? The blindfolded woman outside the courthouse and the public, that's who.

What's worse, plea bargains are sometimes used by overly aggressive district attorneys to get an innocent man to plead guilty to a "reduced charge" when he did not commit any crime in the first place. That way the DA racks up another win with minimal effort. Even in the best light possible, plea bargains are a bad idea and in most cases are a total anathema to justice.

Some people claim that eliminating the plea bargain process would result in utter paralysis of the court system, but in states where plea bargaining has been eliminated such has not occurred. In the few states where the practice has been abolished, DAs only charge what they can prove, eliminating a lot of charges they used to pile on suspects to coerce a plea. When prosecutors only charge what they can prove, it makes them work for their paycheck like most people have to. Plus, they don't waste time haggling and dickering with defendants, so time is actually saved.

• • • • •

There are, I'm certain, many more laws that could be passed or abolished to improve the justice system. The ones I've proposed above are just a start. If you want to protect your rights, start organizing petitions to get them on the ballot in your state's next election.

CHAPTER 12

From Newspeak to Newlaw

The Legalized Erosion of American Liberty

Are you familiar with the term "Newspeak"? Odds are you are not, but you damn well should be, especially in today's world. Asking the pardon of those who are familiar with the term, I will give you a quick education in the term and its relevance to American society at the beginning of the 21st century.

In 1948, a writer named George Orwell wrote a chilling and prophetic novel called *1984*. Wanting to set the novel in the not too distant future, Orwell simply reversed the last two digits of the year he wrote it in, just in case you were wondering.

In *1984*, Orwell envisioned a brutal, totalitarian government called "Big Brother" (where we get the familiar phrase, "Big Brother is watching you), which sought nothing less than absolute control over every citizens' life in minute detail. The best way to control what people think is to control what they hear; the best way to control what people hear is to control what they can say; the best way to control what they say is to control the language; hence Big Brother created the official language for the State and dubbed it Newspeak.

Newspeak was a carefully crafted language in which anything the State didn't want to be said literally could not be said. There were no words for "dissent" or "dissatisfaction" in the Newspeak lexicon, so it was impossible to express disagreement with Big Brother's decisions. Those who insisted on using the verboten Oldspeak were dealt with by the Thought Police until they either got with the program or were rendered incapable of threatening the new order's peace and security.

By controlling what people could say, Newspeak was meant to control what people thought. Thus Newspeak became a perversion of language. The original intent of language was to express ideas and thoughts, to facilitate the exchange of same. Newspeak was meant to stifle ideas and control thought by making it impossible to express those that the State didn't approve of.

As I'm sure some of you have realized, we have our very own form of Newspeak in the United States today. The American version is a mixture of political correctness and official jargon meant to obscure truth and crush dissent. Under American Newspeak, for example, you aren't fired from a job anymore, you are "downsized" or "right sized" or "mutually departed." Sounds nicer than "thrown out of work," doesn't it? Likewise, under American Newspeak rules, some people are allowed to insult and offend anyone they want, publicly and loudly, while others who make "incorrect" remarks in the privacy of their own homes are rooted out and corrected by today's version of the Thought Police.

Yes, Newspeak is alive and well in America. For those of you unfamiliar with it, I suggest you read *1984* and compare what happened in Orwell's imaginary world to what's happening in our real world today. While you're at it, get a copy of *Brave New World* by Aldous Huxley and read it too. You could also rent and watch the movie *Soylent Green*. All three of these stories are increasingly more relevant to America in the 21st century.

Just to prove how well she is, America's version of Newspeak has given birth to a child recently. The offspring's name is "Newlaw," and he's just as foul as his mother, and even more dangerous. Newlaw is to the original purpose and intent of American law what Newspeak was to the original purpose of language. Where language was meant to convey and encourage thought and ideas, Newspeak was meant to control thought and crush ideas.

So it is with Newlaw. The original aim of American law was to enforce justice and protect the rights of the people against threats from all sources. The intent of Newlaw in to enforce injustice and crush the rights of the people under the state's boot. I'll give you a particularly blatant and egregious example of Newlaw. Once you see Newlaw for what it is and understand the concept, I'm sure you'll be able to find more and more examples of it, probably in your own state, city, or town.

In Michigan, lawmakers in some areas are trying to make the court system faster and more efficient by eliminating jury trials altogether. In order to facilitate this, they've used the power of Newspeak to create Newlaw that bypasses many of the most important aspects of American justice and constitutional protections. Here's how they do it:

They've created a new class of "acts" that are not considered crimes. Rather, they're called "civil infractions." Civil infractions, for now, include things like not having your house painted, having weeds in your yard, having unrepaired damage to your property, and so forth. In other words, very minor, petty things.

If someone decides that you've committed a civil infraction, you are notified to correct it within so many days or else.

If the situation has not been corrected to some minor government official's satisfaction, you are notified to appear at a hearing and "show cause" as to why you should not be fined or possibly jailed for contempt. Since you haven't committed a crime but instead just an "infraction," you aren't technically on trial and therefore don't get the same rights and protections as an official criminal would.

Under Oldlaw, you had the option of demanding a trial by jury, even for a misdemeanor, and you were presumed to be innocent unless proven guilty. But under Newlaw, you don't have the option of demanding a trial by jury, or any trial at all, because it's only an "infraction." Furthermore, you are presumed guilty on the say-so of whichever city official made the accusation and must prove yourself innocent before a judge who works for the same city as the person accusing you.

So Newlaw has eliminated the presumption of innocence and the right to a jury trial for civil infractions. Of course if this flies—that is, if the public tolerates it—more and more things will be classed as civil infractions instead of crimes. Again, since you are not being accused of a crime, you won't have the right to a jury trial, presumption of innocence, etc.

The Michigan civil infraction scam isn't the first case of Newlaw in this country. A while back we were given "forfeiture laws" that allowed the system to seize money and property without trial, and if the citizen wanted it back he had to pay court fees to fight for it. Newlaw, in this case, used American Newspeak to disguise what was going on under a transparent rationalization that claimed that the state wasn't seizing property from individuals; rather, the individuals had forfeited the assets in question through presumed (and unproven) criminal activity. Thus forfeiture laws skirted the inconvenient issue of "unreasonable search and seizure" from which American citizens are suppose to be protected by the Constitution.

Some courts have struck down early examples of

Newlaw, and I hope they continue to do so, but I'm cynical enough to think that the crafters of Newlaw will either make more esoteric versions that will slip through the courts while having the same effect on our rights, or they will simply have a little talk with dissenting judges to "get their minds right" on the issue.

There have been cases where Newlaw received the court's stamp of approval too. A few years ago a state seized a man's car while he was soliciting an undercover cop posing as a hooker. Under the state's forfeiture laws, the car became the state's property even though the man's wife owned half of it. Civil rights groups put up a valiant fight, but in the end the courts ruled for the state, effectively allowing it to take property from an innocent person (the wife) without compensation.

I'm not too optimistic about anything anymore. I think the only way to stop the courts from taking more and more freedom away from the public is for the public to stand up and say "NO!" to it and to back it up with force. I just don't know if the public has what it takes to do that anymore.

Who knows? Maybe there is a bright side to the decay of the American judicial system. As it continues to become ever more rancid and putrid, maybe more and more people will have to realize it is what it is and stop relying on it for anything. Then maybe people will start using their own judgement and listening to their own conscience in matters of right and wrong, reawakening ideas like independent thought and personal moral choice. Eventually the public might even get its act together, throw away the current system, and replace it with something better.

This book is a small step in that direction.

CHAPTER 13

Resources in the Information Age

When I was a kid I saw an old movie set in ancient Arabia starring Sabu the jungle boy. Sabu and his friend had found a Djinn (basically a genie on steroids) and were using him to help defeat some evil guy. At one point in the movie, Sabu and his friend were cornered in the evil guy's palace, so they asked the genie to give them the finest weapons he knew of to fight the bad guy's thugs.

The Djinn thinks for a moment and, drawing upon his vast store of knowledge, determines what the finest weapons are. He makes magical gestures at the two heroes and lo! Nothing appears, not even a dagger. When questioned by the startled boys, the Djinn replies he has indeed given them the finest weapons he knows of—wisdom and courage.

I agree with the Djinn's rational here. Wisdom and courage are the best weapons in most situations, especially when fighting tyranny. After all, Mohandas Gandhi drove the British out of India without ever picking up a gun.

While wisdom and courage are perhaps important attributes in the struggle against tyranny, there is another weapon that is nearly as potent and absolutely indispensable.

That weapon is *information.*

Information is a powerful force, in some ways and at some times more powerful than an army. Wars have been won or lost because one side had information that the other did not. The fate of the world could have been changed many times had one bit of information been made available to one person at the right time. Imagine how D-Day may have played out had Hitler only known the exact location of the Allied invasion or the day it would occur.

Tyrants have always known that information is a great power, and virtually every tyrannical regime has worked feverishly to control it. From the Catholic church's suzerainty over Europe in the Dark Ages to government despots in this very day, those who would reign supreme have waged war upon the free flow of ideas and information among the people who they want to control. The Nazis proudly staged mass book burnings in the early heyday of their regime. The Soviets filled gulags with those who spoke openly against communism. And during its short reign in Afghanistan, the Taliban outlawed the printing of newspapers or the possession of televisions in order to isolate the Afghan people from "corrupting" information.

We are very lucky to live in the information age, where technology like computers and the Internet make knowledge and ideas widely available and almost impossible to censor completely. If you are going to make a stand against tyranny, you need to make use of this rich source of power, and in order to do so you must be able to access the Internet so you can tap the resources it offers.

If you don't have a computer, you should get one. Even a used and obsolete model can still access the Net and bring unlimited information to your fingertips. If you can't get a computer or hook up to Internet service, find a computer-savvy friend or relative and ask for his or her help. Also note that almost every public library in America is likely to have some sort of Net access available to the public, and that most community colleges now offer adult education courses in computers and Internet accessing.

The modern man who would stand up for his rights is virtually emasculated without the ability to access the Internet. If you should fall into this category, then you should make empowering yourself a priority.

The following organizations may be of assistance to anyone interested in the topic of jury rights. Visit their Web sites, inform and empower yourself, and remember that many people under tyrannical regimes might have risked death to access a fraction of the information and knowledge that you can acquire with just one evening exploring the Internet. For those of you who do not have Internet access, I have included regular mailing addresses as well. All contact information was current at the time of this book's publication.

The Fully Informed Jury Association (FJIA) is the country's leading advocate for educating American citizens about their rights, powers, and responsibilities as jurors, including the right of jury nullification. Anybody interested in the topic of jury rights must start here.

Fully Informed Jury Association
1900 N. MacArthur Blvd., Suite 227
Oklahoma City, OK 73127
http://www.fija.org/

Citizens for Judicial Accountability (CJA) is a citizens' watchdog group dedicated to raising awareness about "the costs and consequences of real and potential abuses in our civil justice system." The group is working toward restoring the traditional separation of powers in the American courtroom.

Citizens for Judicial Accountability Inc.
8020 N.E 4th Avenue
Miami, Florida 33138
http://www.judicialaccountability.org/

The Jury Rights Project was formed in Colorado to promote and defend the concept that jurors are "the voice of the community" and should be free to acquit or convict defendants as they see fit without fear of retribution from the government. The group is a direct outgrowth of the Laura Kriho prosecution.

Jury Rights Project
P.O. Box 729
Nederland, CO 80466
http://www.levellers.org/jrp/

The Judicial Accountability Initiative Law (J.A.I.L.) is an amendment initiative in California to allow the independent investigation of cases of judicial misconduct and abuse of power.

J.A.I.L.
P.O. Box 207
North Hollywood, CA 91603
http://www.jail4judges.org/

Families Against Mandatory Minimums (FAMM) challenges "inflexible and excessive penalties required by mandatory sentencing laws." FAMM promotes the idea that judges should be once again allowed to use their discretion to determine reasonable sentences so the punishment truly fits the crime.

Families Against Mandatory Minimums
1612 K Street NW, Suite 1400
Washington, D.C. 20006
http://www.famm.org/

The American Civil Liberties Union (ACLU) is the best-known civil rights organization in the United States. They will legally represent defendants in cases where the U.S. government has overstepped its bounds. Be aware that the ACLU receives thousands of requests for legal representation, so there is no guarantee they will choose your case to fight.

American Civil Liberties Union
125 Broad Street, 18th Floor
New York, NY 10004
http://www.aclu.org/

The Institute for Justice (IJ) describes itself as "our nation's only libertarian public interest law firm" that pursues "cutting-edge litigation in the courts of law and in the court of public opinion on behalf of individuals whose most basic rights are denied by the State." Like the ACLU, there are no guarantees the IJ will choose to represent your case over the many others it considers, but they are still worth contacting.

Institute for Justice
1717 Pennsylvania Ave., NW, Suite 200
Washington, D.C. 20006
http://www.ij.org